Laurie Taylor
In the
Underworld

COUNTERPOINT

London
UNWIN PAPERBACKS
Boston   Sydney

First published by Basil Blackwell Publishers Limited 1984
First published in Unwin Paperbacks 1985

Unwin Paperbacks
40 Museum Street, London WC1A 1LU, UK

Unwin Paperbacks
Park Lane, Hemel Hempstead, Herts HP2 4TE, UK

George Allen & Unwin Australia Pty Ltd
8 Napier Street, North Sydney, NSW 2060, Australia

Allen & Unwin Inc
Fifty Cross Street, Winchester, Mass 01890, USA

British Library Cataloguing in Publication Data

Taylor, Laurie
In the underworld——(Counterpoint)
1. Crime and criminals——England——London
2. London (England)——Social life and customs
——20th century
I. Title   II. Series
364.3′09421   HV6950.L7
ISBN 0–04–364022–2

Printed in Great Britain by
Richard Clay (The Chaucer Press) Ltd,
Bungay, Suffolk

Contents

PREFACE AND ACKNOWLEDGEMENTS

All the names of past and present professional criminals in this book, with, of course, the exception of John McVicar, are pseudonyms. Some of the club names – the Newmarket Sporting Club, the Landsdowne, the Professional Artists' Association – are also disguises, although such other well-known places as the French Pub, the Swiss Tavern, L'Escargot, Ronnie Scott's, and the Salisbury retain their proper titles.

I define 'professional criminals' as all those whose livelihood for a period of at least five years has been based primarily on persistent criminal activity. Five years is somewhat arbitrary, but it does just about distinguish between those delinquents for whom crime is a phase and those for whom it becomes a career. In places, I have preferred the term 'villain' to the clumsier 'professional criminal', although I am aware that it is also favoured by criminals themselves who rely on its archaic connotations to give their illegalities a more 'lovable' character.

For a variety of reasons, several forms of professional crime are missing from this six-month tour of London's 'underworld'. Fortunately, there are some excellent recent studies to remedy the most obvious omissions: Michael Levi on long firm fraud (*The Phantom Capitalists*, 1981), Pat Carlen on female professional crime (*Criminal Women*, 1984), Steven Box on corporate crime (*Power, Crime and Mystification*, 1983) and John McVicar himself on police corruption (*The Rotten Orchard*, 1984. Videocassette Falcon, U.K. Ltd).

It was Mary McIntosh's essays on the social organization of crime which prompted my initial interest in the subject, Dick Hebdige's MA dissertation on villainy and style which added some flavour, and the interest and enthusiasm of the journalists and writers named in chapter 7 which helped carry me through a difficult patch in the middle of the research.

As most of the interviews in this book were recorded in noisy public places and featured individuals whose speech was not always readily intelligible to those outside their immediate community, I must pay a particular tribute to Sue Plummer for the intelligent assistance that she provided with some of the transcription.

Portions of this book appeared in a series of articles in *New Society* and I would like to thank the editor Paul Barker for permission to reproduce this material and, as always, for his valuable comments and encouragement.

That leaves John McVicar. I can only hope that the rest of the book makes clear the full extent, as well as the exact nature, of my debt to him.

1

MEETING THE PROFESSIONALS

In which John comes out of prison – the author is taken to his first spieler – learns how to drink properly – and arranges a research project.

It had been a mistake to choose the Salisbury in St Martin's Lane as our first meeting place. I'd had to choose quickly. I'd been writing letters to John McVicar in prison for thirteen years and quite expected to do so for another five. And then the postcard had arrived – written in that familiar cramped handwriting which nearly all prisoners develop to defeat Home Office restrictions on the maximum size of letters: 'I've got parole and will be starting a sociology postgraduate course at Leicester in October. I'll be in London next week. Let's meet. Be lucky. *John McVicar.*' There was even some space left over.

I suppose I thought of the Salisbury because I remembered it from my days as a drama student nearly 20 years before. It had seemed all very bohemian then. We'd pile in from our drama college in Sidcup on a Friday night and stand round in the great baroque bar watching famous actors, and people pretending to be famous actors, going through that dreary limp-wristed *double entendre* chit-chat which passed for conversation in those days. 'Darling you look as though you could do with a fill-up.' 'Well *you* can fill me up any time you like, sweetheart.' It didn't exactly sound like John McVicar's scene, but it would at least let him know straightaway that I was familiar with the West End action and moved easily in deviant circles.

For good measure I also decided to take along Professor Basil Bernstein. I'd been acting as external examiner for Basil that day at the London University Institute of Education and it seemed too good a chance to miss. Every social scientist knows Basil's perceptive work on elaborated and restricted language codes, and John could hardly fail to be impressed. 'I'd love to come,' Basil had said when I explained, with his usual mercurial and slightly camp enthusiasm.

But it was perfectly clear, as soon as Basil and I pushed our way into the saloon bar of the Salisbury just five minutes before the meeting time, that this was far from being the perfect rendezvous. For a start, it was no longer bohemian in the way it had been. The decor looked much the same, although the mirrors looked far too shiny to be the Victorian ones I remembered. But more significant than any environmental change was the ideological renovation. The Salisbury had gone from camp to gay. There was not a limp wrist or silk scarf to be seen, nor a 'sweetheart' or 'darling' to be heard. Instead, men stood around making laconically efficient contact with each other.

It might all have been perfectly tolerable if Basil's usual theoretical sensitivity to the nuances of language had been complemented by some practical sense that 'dearheart' was not the most appropriate form of address in this setting. And if only it hadn't also been necessary for me to keep glancing round in case I failed to recognize John when he arrived. Glancing casually around in this setting was about as innocuous as stroking a torch across brushwood. Every pair of eyes you encountered crackled with interest or animosity.

What did John look like anyway? My memory of him from the class at Durham was confused. For the brief period of time that I'd taught him, he'd been sitting behind a table and I wasn't now sure how much my real memory had been influenced by press reports of his exploits. I had him, though, at about six foot tall, with dark hair. Fortunately it was John – all five foot nine of him, balding, with light brown hair – who recognized me. It wasn't clear whether he was pleased to see me, but I noticed with relief, as we went up to the Lamb and Flag in Long Acre to find some space, that there was no sign, at least as yet, of the 'thin snarling lips' which the *Mirror* had thought so significant in its report of his escape.

It was an uneasy evening, not at all helped by a misunderstanding between Basil and John which effectively laid waste to the content of nearly half an hour of conversation. Basil had with his usual solicitousness enquired about the quality of John's supervision at Leicester University. Like other academics who treat their occupational world as primary he'd simply asked about supervision at Leicester (much as the professor in *Lucky Jim* was inclined to pick up his office phone with the bald pronouncement 'History speaking'). John, unused to such elision, had assumed that the supervision of which Basil spoke was that provided in Leicester by his probation officer. 'You mean you have to get his permission to come to London,' exclaimed Basil in horror, while John insisted that he couldn't complain because his supervisor did at least allow him to have a woman stay overnight in his flat.

But without such troubled beginnings I might not have found myself in the Newmarket Sporting Club later that evening. For John clearly decided at about half-past nine that he wanted something a little less exhausting on his first night back in London than a pub discussion about academic sociology. 'Yeah, well, I'd better be going,' he announced. Basil tactfully took his leave while I hung around until I could leave with John – 'Oh, don't worry, this is more or less my direction,' I said as he moved off towards Cambridge Circus. 'Well, nice to see you after all these years,' I offered in Charing Cross Road. 'You can get such a misleading impression of people from letters. Did you ever read André Gide's *Strait is the Gate*?' Across Oxford Circus. 'Doesn't Broadcasting House look from here like the prow of a vast liner?' And then round the back of Harley Street.

'Come on,' he said. 'I'll show you what a spieler looks like.' He turned into a doorway of a house with a nameplate which advertised 'Osteopathic Services', up two flights of stairs, and there was the Newmarket Sporting Club.

Cigar smoke hung in the air, newspapers lay around on tables and in the corner of the room about fifteen men were absorbed in a noisy game of cards. Only about six actually seemed to be playing: the rest were either spectators or waiting for their turn to get in on the action. It was a difficult game to follow, with sudden moments of stillness followed by quick and noisy flurries during which cards were taken and discarded with a speed which suggested more a boisterous session of snap or strip-jack-naked than any game of skill. 'Kalooki,' explained John, adding rather unhelpfully, 'a sort of Jewish gin rummy.'

It was difficult to know whether to be more surprised by the size of the pile of £10 notes in the kitty in the centre of the table, or by the fact that several of these high-rollers, while evidently playing for Monte Carlo stakes, were pulling on mugs of tea and casually munching bacon sandwiches (evidently kalooki was not that Jewish) as hundred of pounds sped backwards and forwards between them.

For all the bacon butties and chipped mugs, these were clearly successful men. Sharply cut suits and silk shirts. Rolls or 'wedges' of folded money which, when not on display, were carried in the back pocket. Gold jewellery was much in evidence: chunky signet rings and fat gold watches.

We stood well clear of the circle, but John had already been greeted by a couple of people who'd detached themselves from the edge of the action. 'Well done John. Good to see you.' No mention of prison or comments about how long he'd been out or what he was going to do.

'All criminals,' said John quietly during a kalooki flurry. 'All professional criminals.' He went through them for my benefit. 'On the left – he's a hoister. Good at it. On the left of him, I think he's a hoister; I'm not sure.' Over on the right was a con man and sitting next door where we went to pick up tea and our own bacon sandwiches was a couple who were 'at the heavy' (robbers). Later a burglar came in and someone John described as an 'all purpose thief'. In fact, everyone in the place except John and myself seemed to be working criminals.

We stayed around for an hour or so, drinking tea in the back room, while members drifted in from time to time to say hello – or just to give John a firm touch on the shoulders as they passed – a sort of re-entry ritual which seemed the more effective because of its understatement. A couple of conversations took off about what had been going on here and there, and when this happened I affected as much interest as I could in my mug of tea. No one seemed to want to trouble John too much. They all knew how much time he'd done and tacitly respected his probable wish for some space in which to get life started up again. It reminded me of the attitude of team-mates to an injured football star returning for his first game after the lay-off. A few simple passes straight to his feet, but no long through-balls for him to chase.

There were more practical ways of saying 'welcome back'. Although John didn't give me any figure for himself, I learnt later that it is not uncommon for returning villains to pick up three or four thousand pounds from club well-wishers in the days immediately following their release. That sort of money, coupled with the warmth and density of the welcome-home ceremony I'd been witnessing, suggested that ordinary hostel or release schemes designed to keep the professional criminal on the straight and narrow were likely to have a somewhat marginal impact. Finding yourself in this sort of club again after years inside wasn't drifting into evil ways, or mixing with bad company, or yielding to temptations. It was coming home.

Although at the time I knew something about professional

criminals from books and articles, most of the material I'd come across had been based on the imprisoned variety, or upon biographies and autobiographies dealing with characters who for all their earlier deviance were now anxious to stress their present reformation. Nothing I'd read had quite prepared me for the self-confidence and open camaraderie of the crowd at the Newmarket Sporting Club. Neither had I expected the taken-for-granted community of interest which seemed to exist between such different criminals. Although my upper-class contacts had often told me that it was not unusual at their London clubs to find prominent sportsmen, high-court judges, television personalities and senior politicians sharing the same table, this had fitted neatly with my hegemonic analysis of British society. It was rather more disconcerting to find a similar degree of common interest among prominent burglars, hoisters, con men, robbers and gangsters.

Not that these villains were to be found relaxing in armchairs discussing the latest developments in the world of crime. It was a highly volatile place, with people arriving and leaving at a speed which you'd associate more with an airport than a social rendezvous. 'Probably going to work,' John explained when I asked him late into the evening about the rapid turnover. 'It's not nine to five, you know.'

Although I was something of a social embarassment – an outsider whose presence precluded intimacies about who'd 'had it off' recently, and where, and how much – I felt that he was glad to have me around for his reunion evening. He positively enjoyed some of my clumsy efforts to understand the scene. 'All this gambling', I'd insisted, 'fits in with Walter Miller's work on the emphasis upon fatalism in the working class.' (Not to mention my misunderstanding: I'd asked him early on, with a vision of rock-breaking in mind, if being 'at the heavy' meant doing time in prison.) Perhaps my straight, gauche presence also reminded him that he had now decided to hold himself a little apart from this stylish, enticing, criminal culture. He'd done enough prison: he wasn't going to go back again. This didn't mean, as I was to hear him say a hundred times, that he no longer acknowledged or respected criminal values and attitudes, or that he'd 'gone straight' or reformed. it simply meant that he was no longer 'active'. Altogether, I felt confident enough to ask him if he'd take me to other clubs, let me see more of this society. On our early-morning stroll back to Oxford Street to find a taxi, he agreed. Tomorrow afternoon. Two-ish. We'd meet in the bar of a hotel in the Bayswater Road and go on to a spiel run by a friend of his in Notting Hill.

This time it was the basement, and the gold plaque said Professional Artists' Association. We allowed ourselves to be checked over by a camera in the lobby, and strolled into a luxurious version of the Newmarket. There was a smart cocktail bar, a couple of gaming-tables and a few armchairs. In the far corner of the room a television flicked between channels in pursuit of the day's race meetings, while an Extel commentary occasionally broke the silence with its familiar laconic phrases – 'Going down Kempton. . . . Under orders Kempton. . . . Off at Kempton.'

Under the television set, at a large table decorated with nothing more than a midday *Standard*, a man was phoning through substantial bets for the half a dozen 'professional artists' who were clustered around him.

The big attraction in these spiels was the non-tax bet. You gave your selection to the man and he passed it through to a central bookmaker who handed over any winnings with only a three per cent deduction instead of the ten per cent which the normal punter would have to pay. That three per cent deduction which the bookmaker creamed off could then come back to the club as commission for the business which had been put his way. As far as I could tell, all this involved some active collusion with big-time bookmakers. While small bets could be handled by local people, larger ones would have to be laid off, and that meant some non-recording and, therefore, tax evasion by major bookmakers, who wanted to hang on to such profitable accounts.

I also learnt you could jack up your winnings a little more by getting the man in the club to bargain for better odds. So if, for example, one of the 'professional artists' had a 'grand' to stake, he might find that the 5 to 1 showing on the television screen or in the Extel commentary could be shifted a point to 6 to 1. It all made betting a bit more personal: you could get yourself a bargain.

That was important. For as I was also to discover, the professional criminal – like the very rich – stakes a lot of his status on not paying the proper price for anything. There's always an angle, some little racket into which he can slip, which makes each transaction – whether what's at stake is a racing bet, a restaurant meal, or a ticket to a rock concert – a confirmation of his position as an insider.

Down at the Newmarket and the Professional Artists' and the other clubs I visited in the next few days, it wasn't just the untaxed bets and the preferential odds which provided the nice sense of being a little bit cleverer than the rest of the world; there was also a lot of talk about this and that jockey and trainer, and how the odds were moving on the course. The fact that there were likely to be people around who'd recently had a drink with the jockey in question, and had had some practical experience of manipulating odds at actual courses, added to the seriousness of it all. It was all a far cry from Joe Soap down the road at Ladbrokes with his list of *Sun* selections and his £1 each way. There is no coincidence in the fact that the standard phrase among professional criminals for the victim of their illegal operations is 'mug punter', the lowest of all beings, a person who gambled without ever realizing how the odds had been cunningly stacked against him. Professional criminals gambled heavily, some did little else between jobs, staying up at clubs like the Newmarket and the Professional Artists' for sessions lasting up to 48 hours and casually losing several thousand pounds. But they always had to feel that they were in complete control. Whatever they did when they were gambling was a reflection of their character, and nothing else. The decisions were all theirs. No one was taking them. They knew the odds.

Of course, the clubs took a cut of the proceeds. But spielers and drinking clubs for criminals are not first and foremost get-rich-quick outfits. They serve as many social and welfare functions as masonic lodges: home-coming criminals, and wives and children of departing criminals can expect a handout: interest-free credit seems permanently available. Even routine loans are, in this company, quite substantial. I remember John asking me one evening if I could lend him some cash. 'Yes, sure.' I was mentally preparing for a fiver. After all, I usually carried about £25 in my wallet so as to be ready for such an emergency. 'Two hundred would be handy,' he said. That sort of money, in little rolls of high denominations, passed hands in clubs with no more comment or sign of record-keeping than would be attached elsewhere to a round of cigarettes. I heard Dave talking about it one night in the Newmarket. I'd been unable to keep my face straight when he'd mentioned the need to get his hands on a couple of grand in the next few days to satisfy one of his creditors. He caught my look and I stuttered something about it being quite a lot to owe. To John's delight, he used the occasion to rub home the sustaining nature of the criminal culture in which he spent his life:

'I haven't gone through three years – John'll tell you – without owing in one given week between £14,000 and £18,000. About 18 grand now. Right? It's absolutely true. You wouldn't believe it. *Aren't I privileged to be able to do that? Aren't I privileged to be able to do that for three years? That's the sort of people I know.* So. No collateral. No bank accounts. Nothing.'

An efficient credit system seemed to be vitally necessary to professional criminals because of the vagaries of fortune which their trade entailed. If people had had 'one off' recently, had pulled a stroke, then they would be spoken of as 'having money'. Those who hadn't had such luck recently – even if they had several hundred in their back pocket – were 'out of money'. That was Dave's state at the moment: 'I haven't had money for four or five months. The only time I've had three or four grand, it's because other people are tut-tutting. When I'm in debt, I know I've got to go out and do a bit. But I haven't had money for four months.'

You can only operate such a sustaining and elaborate credit system in a stable world. And the clubs provided just the necessary foundation. The gambling upon which they rest – the gambling which is so inextricably linked to professional crime – might get you on a roller-coaster which meant you needed yet another lump of money to pay off the debt which you'd run up when hazarding the last big haul. But everything else about the place was rock-solid. A gangster was on hand in most clubs to provide a little background pressure, but there was no sense that anything was likely to be disturbed by outside forces, that the door was about to burst open to admit a horde of armed policemen.

Only a few reminders of the rule of law outside ever seemed to insinuate themselves. One or two people, for example, would be conspicuous by their sudden absence from the Kalooki table or the bar. But such temporary departures were hardly mentioned. Among active villains, prison is about as likely a topic for extended conversation as lung cancer at Imperial Tobacco.

Neither did there seem much evidence of a hierarchy among the club members; although it was known who'd 'had money' recently and who hadn't. At the Professional Artists', a couple of gangsters could sometimes be seen holding court from high stools positioned at strategic points along the bar, but otherwise, rather as in actors' clubs, it was a point of etiquette *not* to recognize people until it was clear they wanted such acknowledgement. Nobody in the Newmarket or the Professional Artists' or the Landsdowne Bridge Club (a favourite of mine) ever rushed up exclaiming, 'Why, Blonde Harry! Long time no see.'

John seemed pleased at the effect that his conducted tour of all these clubs was having on me. He did draw back a little when I started slapping sociological interpretations around the place: he was not too impressed, for example, with my view that the professional criminal's idea of the good life (champagne, cigars, fat rolls of notes, gold watches) was essentially working class. But he seemed to like it when I marvelled at the orderliness and coherence and naturalness of it all. Perhaps, after all those probation officers and assistant governors who'd come up with lines like, 'But surely John, an intelligent man like you can't allow yourself to be caught up in such a self-defeating, immoral enterprise as that,' it was a relief to him to have a sociologist in tow who could at least sense the attraction of it all.

He usually introduced me as 'Laurie', accompanied by a single nod of the head, which I took to mean 'not one of us but all right'. Not that there was ever any chance of my being confused with the usual clientele. Wherever we went, I stood out like a spare prick. My 6 feet 2 inches put me a good three inches above everyone else and there was something wrong with the shape and the weight of my head, body, hands and feet. I felt too loosely integrated and insubstantial, as though I was hanging from the ceiling, like a left-over Christmas decoration, rather than being firmly rooted to the floor.

My greatest embarassment was always reserved for the moments when I attempted to buy a round of drinks. I knew about rounds all right. I could keep a careful watch on whose turn it was, and spot the moment when the level of the drink in the glasses was just low enough to warrant a refill. But I would keep fiddling with single pound notes in order to assemble the heavy cost of the round – sometimes £10 or more could disappear with one order – while everyone else seemed to deal exclusively in twenties and fifties. Worst of all (at least for the first half-dozen visits), I still believed it manly to order pints of bitter. There I'd be, tall and gangly with my pint mug of McEwans Export Keg, while all around were squat mesomorphic villains, with shoulders so broad and strong that I could have rested my elbows on them, sipping their Bacardis and vodkas. Pints, I eventually learnt, were definitely downmarket in these surroundings. They smelt of bingo and the *News of the World* and darts and dominoes and chips and knees-ups and a hundred and one other bits of working-class life which were just about as conversationally taboo in this company as a reference to the grand job being done at present by the Old Bill. I remember arriving one afternoon at the Landsdowne with Dave and John and offering to get the round in while Dave went off to make a phone call. 'Watcha want, Dave?' I asked.

'Bacardi. Yes, Barcardi,' he said: 'or vodka.' Then, with a sudden recollection of my own tastes, 'Nothing drecky like real ale.'

'Drecky?'

'Shit,' said John.

Not that the people at the clubs were ever rude to me. If they wanted to talk a little more intimately to John, they'd move him slightly to the side by cupping a conspiratorial hand under his elbow. Down at the Newmarket one September afternoon, a man who was in charge of rather more cashmere sweaters than personal use might warrant on such a warm day, actually excused himself for not bringing me in on the conversation. 'Look, Lol,' he said solicitously as he moved John away, 'I'm sorry about all this. But this is business talk. Just like you have at the University. I expect.' I nodded enthusiastically.

· 'I suppose', I said to John one night, as we made our way back from the Professional Artists', about three weeks after our first absurd meeting in the Salisbury, 'they're not all that different to accountants or stockbrokers. I can see what you mean about it being a job to them. They get up in the morning, or at least in the afternoon, and go to work. Keep their eyes open. Look for openings. And I suppose just like other professional groups they pull together their own set of attitudes and ideas about what's right and wrong, about how to have a good time, how to treat their families and kids, how to look after other people who're in the same game.'

It was a prepared speech. I left out the bits that I didn't think John would like to hear. It was all very well for me to talk about crime as an occupation like any other, but I also knew that the well-dressed men jiggling ice in their double Bacardis and triple vodkas in the Landsdowne Bridge Club had, not long previously, been out on the streets, cheating and stealing, selling drugs and threatening violence. Whenever they'd been working, they'd had to go about it surreptitiously with forged papers or keys, at night or in disguise. There would nearly always have been a victim, not necessarily left bleeding in the gutter, but often left injured or distressed or corrupted or shamefaced.

But I kept quiet about all that. I could come back to the anti-social and immoral aspects of it all. At the moment I just wanted to find out how successful professional criminals went about their business, how they organized particular 'coups', learnt their techniques, integrated their work with home and family, dealt with long-term imprisonment. I wanted to know how they got into this way of life, and how they got out of it. Most of all, I wanted to understand why it had such a continuing appeal for a group of people who in every way seemed a million miles from the standard picture of the dull-witted persistent offender.

'John?' We were back now at my flat in Battersea – sitting

across the kitchen table from each other and drinking cups of tea from separate pots. (John insisted upon making his own.) 'John. How would it be if you set up some interviews with top villains and I came along and recorded them, and then we got together and wrote something about it which could give a different perspective from some of the other books on professional crime? We could call it, say, *The Subculture of Professional Crime*.

I'd rehearsed that as well, but it seemed to take less time than I'd planned. John nodded his head slowly and drank some more of the brown sludge he liked to call 'proper tea'.

'We'll try,' he said. 'But you've got to promise something.'

I was poised to agree to anything. No discussion of John's own criminality? Absolute confidentiality when real crimes were mentioned? Complete anonymity for all the interviewees? We shouldn't have too much difficulty in agreeing. We were both sociologists.

'Of course. Of course.'

'Then please, Laurie, will you promise never again to use that fucking word "subculture"?'

2

ROBBING BANKS WITH A PEN

*In which the author meets two con men – develops some
sympathy for Frankie Vaughan – stumbles on villains off to
work – and learns how to pass stolen cheques.*

It was Sunday lunchtime when John rang through to my flat
in Battersea with news of our first contact. I was busy at the
time, marking essays on the causes of delinquency.

'It's the con man from the Angel that I told you about.
Mainly credit cards and TCs.' He paused. I knew why. 'TCs
– that's travellers cheques,' he added. He was finding it
difficult providing this running glossary for me. Nothing
made him angrier than those books by ex-cons with titles like
Doing My Bird or *Frame-up* which included such helpful
information in the glossary as: '*J. Arthur*. Prison slang for
"masturbation". Derivation: rhyming slang from J. Arthur
Rank – Wank.' But at least for the time being I got to know
what TCs were. I made a note.

The idea was that he'd pick me up in Battersea and we'd
then drive over to the 'meet' – a pub in King's Cross. I looked
at my watch. It was 2.15. On a Sunday. 'We'll never make it,'
I pointed out. 'It'll be closed by the time we get there.'

When we finally parked near the Horse and Groom, me
with much shunting backwards and forwards down a side-
street about five minutes' walk away, and John with two
tyres on the pavement outside the frosted glass announcing
SALOON, I felt justified in my concern. The doors were
firmly locked and you couldn't see any bodies, as I'd already
learned to call them, moving around behind the windows.
None of this seemed to bother John, who just kept his finger
on a side-bell next to a poster advertising a benefit to raise

money to send local pensioners to Clacton for what appeared to be an indeterminate period of time, and waited. It took 30 seconds for the bolts to be trundled back, and the door to be opened by a sightly bizarre-looking man who, immediately he recognized John, went into an elaborately overdeferential routine which left him sandwiched behind the door as we strolled through.

It was one of those huge open-plan pubs which only seem to make sense as part of some architect's life-long fight against a snug bar. In the middle of the empty arena, and looking rather like a beleaguered carousel, sat the circular bar with its rows of optics sparkling like organ pipes. I followed John across the Tandoori-red carpet and was introduced to Les, the owner, who now, out from behind the door, was bringing his deferential routine to a close by scuttling alongside John and ushering him towards a stool at the bar.

'Ah, Graham,' he said to me as we shook hands. 'Any pal of John's is a pal of mine.' Somehow, during the introductions, he'd got my name wrong. I should have corrected him at the time, but it didn't seem quite 'subcultural' to do so when he'd just let me into his pub after hours. I decided to stay as Graham for the moment. Perhaps, after all, it was a sort of compliment: exact names weren't likely to be too important in this world of shifting identities and cultivated aliases. But I could have wished for some little more colourful name to set alongside all the other characters I was to hear about – Manchester George, Mad Paddy, Crazyman Bimbo. Something a little racier than plain Graham.

As Les wandered off to the corner of the bar to operate the DJ equipment, I was introduced to our contact, who was perched on another stool at the bar, sipping white wine. Pale-faced, thin, good-quality hounds-tooth jacket, brown daks-style trousers, brown shoes with a thin gold buckle. A representative, I thought to myself. Travelling in something fairly refined. Books perhaps. But good books. Say the Home Counties rep. for Hamish Hamilton. As 'one of the best con men in the country', he was disappointing. He looked, well, altogether too much like nobody but himself.

'Laurie – Geoff,' said John.

'This is quite reasonable,' said Geoff, pulling a bottle of 1979 Sancerre from the ice-bucket near his elbow.

'Mmm,' we agreed. 'Mmm.'

I was rather anxious to get the 'Helloing' and 'Mmming' out of the way as quickly as possible so that I might at last press the record button on the micro-cassette machine and lead into some such questions as: 'Well, Geoff, tell me, how did you first get into bank fraud.' But I got no further with any sort of conversation for suddenly Mick Jagger was Getting – No – Sa – Tis – Fak – Shun through the six coffin-sized speakers stacked high around the room.

'Tho' – I try – and I try – and I try.' Les boogied out of the DJ booth riding the sound like a surfer. When he finally beached up against the bar, he stuck a long finger in my chest and prodded hard. 'You're sixties music, Graham. I can tell.' Les was in a Fiorucci tee-shirt, low-slung jeans, and sneakers. Balanced precariously on the back of his head, at an angle I recalled from Sinatra's 'Wee Small Hours', was a dirty grey trilby.

He turned sharply away, elbow first, disco-style, and began dancing back to the DJ cubicle. Then suddenly sachayed back to me. 'Eh, Graham, I'm a Cherokee Indian. A fucking Cherokee Indian. Know how you can tell?' I did my best to look just a little laconic – sort of 'Battersea Graham' at least. He answered his own question with a degree of satisfaction which seemed unfounded. 'Easy. The fucking *hat*. The *fucking hat*.'

He go-goed back to the turn-table: the Stones gave way to Springsteen, (A close friend of Les's, I was to learn later. Well, in a way. He'd got back-stage at the last Springsteen concert — bouncers and villains have an interchangeability which always makes this sort of access possible — and as Springsteen had come sweating off stage, Les had simply moved forward. 'Well done, Bruce baby. You remember me. *Les*.' 'Oh yes. Hello, Les. Thanks a lot. Can you make the party tonight?' And as luck would have it, Les could just find the time.)

Back at the bar, Geoff was already belying his Hamish Hamilton image by lighting up a ready-rolled joint. I confined myself to hoping that John's probation officer was a long way off. This was a recall offence.

Not that it was exactly a party scene. Two other men were drinking what looked like champagne at the far end of the bar, occasionally mouthing phrases through the wall-to-wall Springsteen, while behind the bar, three barmaids washed, polished, and replenished stocks. What was important for John, Geoff, Les and for the other faces who slowly drifted in, was being there. Being around in a place which was now their own.

Criminals, like the actors I'd occasionally run across in Gerry's Bar in Shaftesbury Avenue or the Kismet in Newport Street, were, it seemed, only properly comfortable when they felt that the straights — anyone who was a potential victim of their art or villainy — had deserted the scene. After a hard day's work robbing banks or treading boards, there was nothing nicer than to relax among a crowd of people who thoroughly credit your reputation, but choose largely to ignore it.

But there was something else about this setting and the behaviour of those within it, which reminded me of the actors' clubs I'd stumbled into during my brief, inglorious career as a professional actor, back in the sixties. It was a sort of old-fashioned bohemianism — a dressing up in slightly bizarre clothes, funny hats, overconventional sports jackets — but most of all a calculated tolerance of each other's eccentricities. As though, this was a sort of ante-room where those who spent their professional lives dissembling in some way or another, pretending to be Hamlet or Ophelia, or pretending *not* to be Armed Robber, Burglar or Con Man, could try out a few little routines without anyone else calling them – Geoff as the Wine Connoisseur, Les as the Waiter, Impessario, and DJ. The feeling grew as other 'acts' arrived to join the company – two men wearing gangster suits who went into an immediate huddle at the far end of the bar and drank their way through a line of Pils bottles and then left as suddenly as they'd arrived. Or a thin, languid youth whom I thought might be police – although not quite enough for me to raise the matter with anyone. He leant on the Space-Invaders machine and sipped Britvic orange with a degree of caution more appropriate to absinthe. Nobody interfered with anyone else's act.

But it was also becoming clear that those like me who had no act were likely to find themselves cast as stooge in other people's routines. Les was back once again. Next to me at the bar. Now into a Jimmy James drunk act with elbow lurching dangerously near to the wine glasses, legs wobbling. Then, the next moment, perfectly in control again, into a slick Travolta routine, and back to the cubicle to segue records on the twin turntable, from Springsteen to Dylan, with all the adroitness of a professional jock.

It seemed that everyone in our little group was happy to let Les have his head, even if the volume of his music coupled with his frequent and alarming bits of play-acting meant any conversation, let alone interviewing, was impossible. It was all worthwhile – or so John sought to assure me – because sooner or later we'd get a good story. For Les didn't just tell other people's tales, he created his own: manufactured a world that was exciting and varied enough for his manic personality. He wasn't just a superb con man, like Geoff, but a sort of impressario of happenings.

At that moment, I noticed with relief, he'd decided I was no longer any fun, and was rounding on John.

'Eh, listen, John. Did you see Diana Dors in that *Escape from the Grave* last night on the telly?'

John had to admit he'd missed it. He'd been trying to fall in love with someone over in South Kensington (all part of what he liked to call 'making up for all those lost years').

'Then I'll tell you something John. That was the greatest film since *Lassie*. No, hold on John. I won't say that. I'll give it a right gee [a boost – a gee-up]. Listen, this is even better.'

He looked around for a second, delaying the argument which would force us all to admit that, when it came to film criticism, he was king.

'Listen.'

We waited.

'Just in case you don't trust my judgement, let me show you what kinda judge of a film I am.'

Go on, said John's face.

'I write my own dialogue, right?'

John nodded. I nodded.

'But I not only write it. I act it, direct it and produce it. That's what kinda judge I am. *And top that.*'

It was a serious challenge. John wasn't inclined to accept. He knew a great deal about Les's dramatic virtuosity – his capacity for scripting real life. There was, for example, the little number known as 'Les and Frankie Vaughan' – a story I was eventually to hear, after much persuasion, from another con man, called Michael.

Apparently, over the years Les had developed a terrible and, as far as I could ever gather, a quite irrational antipathy to Frankie Vaughan. (I suppose if you took a rather Dickensian attitude, you could suspect that all that work the singer did with boys' clubs was seen by Les as depriving the underworld of suitable apprentices.) Anyway, Les went along to see Frankie Vaughan at the Talk of the Town – the club which used to stand on the same site as the new Hippodrome club, at the corner of Charing Cross Road and Leicester Square. He wasn't there, however, to bone up on the lyrics of 'Green Door' or 'Give me the Moonlight', but to work out a plan. He noticed on his visit that during the famous 'Moonlight' number Frankie Vaughan came down off the stage and walked along shaking hands with all the punters sitting at tables by the stage. All you had to do to get a handshake was to be near the front and put out your hand. That was good enough for Les. Next night he was back again. Ringside seat. Champagne. But instead of the ice-bucket staying at the table, it went down at the side of Les's chair, and throughout the second half of Frankie's act – twenty minutes – Les sat stoically with his naked right hand buried up to the wrist in packed ice. Came the 'Moonlight' number and the star, microphone in left hand, took his customary stroll. Across the stage, down the steps, round the front of the auditorium.

'Give me a shady nook,' he warbled, leaning over to shake hands with the delighted customers, 'And leave the rest to me' – and there was Les on his feet in front of him, face beaming with pleasure, right hand eagerly extended. 'Give me a shady ... Aaargh ... nook...' And then it was back on stage for the last number, which had to be sung to an audience which must have seemed to consist of little else but Les's broad, expansive, victorious smile.

That smile was now punting a third bottle of Sancerre down the counter towards us. I decided that I might salvage something from the afternoon by at least chatting up Geoff enough to ensure a long searching interview in some quieter place. 'Good stuff,' I said, making certain to let the wine wash a little over my tongue before swallowing it.

'Pleasant,' he said judiciously.

I began to wonder if a con man knowing more about wine than a professor was a bit subversive of the proper social order. Then I started to think that perhaps Geoff had read my original intention and played a clever double-bluff. Maybe he knew far less about wine than even I did. I was saved from having to choose by Les suddenly demanding complete silence. 'Here you are, Graham,' he announced, peering out of his disco booth like the driver of a steam loco from his tender. The six speakers hissed their warning of the decibels that waited for us. 'Your sort of music. Sixties music, Graham.'

A click like thunder as the stylus engaged the disc. It was quite the loudest version that I have ever heard of 'Paddy McGinty's Goat'.

I've no doubt I could have found my car quite easily after this noisy and completely fruitless afternoon – a cassette and a half of nothing much more than shrieks of pointless laughter and selections from *The Stones Greatest Hits* – if only I hadn't felt so very paranoid. But wandering round the derelict side-streets, many of which looked to my jaundiced eyes as though they'd been the object of saturation bombing within the last fortnight, I couldn't get away from the feeling that unspecified criminals were even now plotting to get me.

Not that there'd been very many likely candidates in the bar as the afternoon drifted away to the sound of Marvin Gaye: just Geoff, the young man drinking Britvic, Les and John, a couple of people who John referred to as 'all-purpose thieves', and the two men drinking Pils who'd looked so much like gangsters – all double-breasted Italian suits and squared shoulders – that it seemed naïve to ask (and anyway was 'gangster' the word you used).

But now I'd certainly got the idea that criminals were everywhere: setting up 'little jobs', arranging 'meets'. And now it seemed they'd stolen or maliciously concealed my Datsun. The Violet. With all the maps of Yorkshire and *The Good Hotel Guide* and – yes, now I remembered – Helen's tennis racquet.

Looking back, I have to blame the marijuana for that unhappy, wandering hour. Up till about four o'clock I'd been congratulating myself on the way I'd stayed sober – 'no more for me, thanks Geoff' – but about then the joints had started circulating. I don't know where they came from; I saw no one rolling. In fact the chain along which they passed didn't seem to have a beginning; it wound backwards and forwards and behind and over the bar like a Mobius strip. But certainly, every couple of minutes, a thumb and index finger with a hand-rolled cigarette pinched between them would move into my line of vision and wait there immobile until I removed the joint. Not a word, not a look, not a pause in the conversation. It all proceeded with the disembodied precision of a mid-air refuelling exercise. I'd only taken a couple of puffs – a bit of vague sucking and blowing was sufficient for most of the time – but it was quite enough for me to get terribly tangled up in a conversation about Tamla Motown, to make me completely forget who recorded 'Tears of a Clown', although only seconds before I'd declared it to be, in a voice that seemed to grow in volume as it moved through the phrase, 'the greatest single record of ALL TIME'.

At least, I thought, as I drove the newly found Violet towards home at a very careful 15 m.p.h., there was another chance for the interview tomorrow morning. John had fixed a 'meet' at Geoff's house in Swiss Cottage at 9.30.

I was only about five minutes late for it despite the morning traffic in the Edgware Road and the need to stop off for some extra cassettes for the micro-recorder. Just in case. But by the time I got to Geoff's front gate, John was already on his way out with two fellows dressed in quiet executive suits, nice polished black shoes and very businesslike expressions. Geoff and Les? Yes it was. I walked quickly towards them. 'You're looking good today.' Dear old Geoff. Good old Les. All that nice wine we'd had together – and the stories – and the music – and the dope. 'Going for an interview?' I asked. (We always say that in the department when anyone turns up in a suit.) I smiled. There I was, ready for interviewing. In my three-piece corduroy suit. With a cassettte-recorder dangling from my right hand.

John glared at me. Gave me what I came to think of as his 'McVigour' look. Geoff and Les wheeled away without any sign of recognition and set off down the street.

'For Christ's sake, Laurie. Can't you see what's going on?'

'What?'

'*They're going to work.*'

'Oh!'

'I got it straight away. As soon as I rang the bell. There was all this fumbling before Geoff opened the door.'

John was furious with me for crashing into them with my lunatic remark, but even more annoyed it seemed with the way in which his involvement in my silly research project had led him to go ringing door-bells in the early morning. Morning – early morning – was the favourite time for the police to come calling. You had only seconds when that happened. Perhaps vital seconds to get a stolen cheque book or a wad of credit cards on the fire. Then, a quick 'Who's there?' and some exchange through the door ('Who d'you say you were?') might gain an extra moment. But that was it. The police on these raids liked kicking doors down: it made the trip worthwhile. It was all so traumatic that friends who were likely to come calling in the early morning approached the door with a proper tentativeness; the milkman had actually been taken aside and lectured on the connection between early-morning bell-pushing and health. His health.

It didn't matter at all that John had made an 'appointment' – was 'expected'. Social arrangements in this culture were vague promissory notes. So much so, that on several occasions I found people showing great surprise at John and me appearing in a particular spot at a particular time, even though an arrangement to do so had been made. 'Hello, John.

Fancy you coming tonight. And ... er ... Graham ... Laurie ... How've you been?'

When John had finally got inside the flat, he'd found Geoff and Les sitting with a wad of traveller's cheques, and practising the signature on their owner's driving licence which would be used as identification. It wasn't just a question of Les getting the signature right, but of learning it by heart. A bank-teller doesn't have to be a detective to realize that something is wrong when the customer who is signing starts glancing across at his own signature for confirmation of the way it goes. And this one had apparently been difficult. The 'G' had a tricky down stroke which was holding them up. Time was critical. The TCs and the driver's licence which they had in front of them were stolen the night before from a hotel in Southampton Row by someone who regularly brought this sort of work to them.

The division of labour was strict. Geoff and Les didn't steal from individuals. They were on the con. But they had regular contacts with hotel thieves and worked on a 'down the middle' basis. If a thief came up with, say, £2000 worth of TCs and some accompanying identification – licence or passport – then he could count on £1,000 for his efforts. But everything fell down unless Geoff and Les could cash the TCs before the banks got the news of their disappearance – got them on their 'list'. John explained that there was no 'big deal' about today's piece of work. It was routine business. Nobody saw it as anything other than a way of getting some bread-and-butter money to last the day, say £500 each for Les and Geoff to use as gambling money when they went down to the spieler in time for the first race. Professional criminals need to tick over between big jobs, get some spending money so they can keep happy while they're waiting for that special bit of business to turn up: the one which will finally allow them to get out of the game altogether; the one which will be big enough to buy the 'little spot' they've always wanted.

(Ironically perhaps, the most favoured 'little spot' for criminals who elaborate these emigration fantasies is Australia.)

'That's all very well, *Professor* Taylor, but why didn't you let the police know that a crime was about to be committed?'
'Well, you see, *I* thought that . . .'
'Surely, you were aiding and abetting?'
'Oh no. Not really. You see, I was just standing there in the street.'
'Your presence was quite enough to give encouragement. "Look", they could say to themselves. "How can this be wrong? Here's a Professor of Criminology, standing by and watching us get on with it!"'
'Well, I can only say . . .'
All this was last November, after a talk in Nottingham at a college of higher education. I was sitting, uncomfortably, in a corner of a seminar room, while some visiting policemen who'd been at my lecture took it in turns to complain about my romanticism – my complicity.
Eventually I managed to produce an answer. 'Look, they'd have commited the crime anyway. Whether I'd have been there or not. They completely ignored me. Looked through me. I couldn't have stopped them if I'd wanted to. And if I had reported the matter to the police, it wouldn't have led to their detection. I had no idea where they were going or whose cheques they were carrying. By the time they were found, they'd have been clean. What's more, any such call to the police would have meant the end of the project. Absolutely no more introductions by John and so no chance whatsoever to discover anything of interest about the tactics and style of a group of criminals about whom we know so little.
'What's more, what's more it wasn't as though anyone was going to get hurt. The whole point about traveller's cheques is that the owner is quickly and fully compensated when they

go missing. Banks themselves are well able to stand the loss: not only do they charge for the travellers cheque service, but of course they make substantial revenue from the short-term investment of all the hard cash they get from the sale of the cheques. So naturally they wish to keep them as attractive as possible by making them so easy to use. The fact that illegitimate users find them almost as readily negotiable is just a small cost to set against the overall benefits. If I also tell you that this was the only time I was ever in a position like this during twelve months of research, wouldn't you say that this one small incident might be condoned. Wouldn't you?'

But unfortunately, by the time I'd put all that together, the policemen had long since gone home, and I was at least half way round the Doncaster by-pass on the way back to York.

It was on Friday of that first week that John warned me about being fatuous. We were setting off again towards Swiss Cottage for our rearranged meet with Geoff. 'You sound so fucking silly,' he complained. 'Always putting in those clever little comments. Why don't you listen a bit more and keep quiet until you've got something to say? And don't keep expecting me to be sociological all the time; these are my friends.'

I stared miserably ahead; immobilized in the position I always took up in the passenger seat when John was driving; body slumped well down into the seat so that my eyeline was heavenward and couldn't readily be invaded by any sudden close-ups of the cars he relentlessly slipstreamed; legs stretched well forward so that my feet could strain against the chassis and avoid any suggestion of the vicarious braking he so despised.

Keeping quiet was easy enough when you were being driven by John. Near misses, or rather near hits, occurred so frequently that for fear of my speech sounding too jumpy or disjointed, I was in the habit of constructing in advance brief phrases containing no more than three or four words. These could then be lobbed in at moments when the next harrowing incident seemed far enough away to allow it: like when we turned into a long straight road with no obvious pedestrian, vehicular, or architectural impediments. 'Must get my hair cut,' I'd go as languidly as possible, while John smacked the long-suffering TI through the gears.

Geoff was at home. In a silk dressing gown. At three o'clock in the afternoon. With a bottle of Dom Perignon in an ice-bucket placed by the side of the big squashy settee which we all plumped into after the introductions.

'All right, John? All right, Graham?'

'Actually it's Laurie. Les kept calling me Graham the other day. But it's Laurie. Laurie Taylor. Lorry Trailer as they used to call me at school.'

That got a glare from John. 'Shall we get started, Geoff,' he said. 'Laurie's got to be off fairly soon.'

The second-floor mansion flat had a great deal of rather new and expensive-looking furniture ranged around it. But it was difficult to detect any uniformity of style. An art deco coffee-table squatted in front of the enveloping Laura Ashley settee; while to the left a Scandinavian light pine dining-table and chairs were placed uneasily alongside a dark oak bookcase. As I was to learn later, much of this stylistic anarchy owed more to the contingencies of hoisting (shop-lifting) than any lack of taste. Geoff took what he was offered; and whether the unintending donor was Maples, Habitat or Heals, it was hardly an occasion for the exercise of judgement. Loot was loot.

I unpacked the cassette-recorder on the glass and tubular steel coffee-table, plugged in the microphone, checked battery and recording levels and then, leaning over John because he was sitting between us, asked Geoff the very first interview question. According to my notes, it was: 'Geoff.

How long would you say you've been a professional criminal?' He promptly stood up.

'Look Laurie. I'll tell you. You'll have to go a bit slow. I mean, I hear a question ... I hear a fucking question like: "Well, Geoff," or "Now then, Geoff," and I'm away. I mean, I associate questions with trouble. That's right isn't it John? Guilty pleas. And that's something I never do. "Nothing to say, Nothing to say. Nothing to say." Right down the sheet. That's my way.'

'But how d'you get started in the business?' said John. I knew it was costing him a lot to press Geoff that way; it was the first in a long list of costs which was eventually to lead to a real crisis about his whole involvement in the project. But for the moment, I was delighted to see that it had brought Geoff down to earth – back to the settee – within range of the microphone.

'I was on the whiz.'

'Pickpocketing?' questioned John, for my benefit.

'Yes. We used to work the Underground. I went down. But it drove me mad. I used to come up full of soot. You'd be down there for hours. You used to come up black. You used to have soot up your nose and it was ... terrible.' He cringed at the memory. Geoff's present fastidiousness could no more tolerate days prowling around the entrails of the Central and the Piccadilly lines than it could cheap brands of champagne.

'That's something I'll never do now, John. I'll never steal from the average person. Right? Something I'd never do. D'you get my meaning?'

In fact, even while pickpocketing, he'd rarely done any actual stealing from an average person. Geoff had nearly always worked as the 'stall' in the gang. It was the 'hook' who did the final removal of the wallet or purse, which on the face of it, seemed much the harder task. But as I slowly got to realize, a good stall was the key to the whole enterprise. The job ranks far higher than the other roles in the division of labour: whereas the robbery may be the *coup de grâce*, it is the complicated ballet of feints and counter-feints carried out beforehand by the stall which ensures the ease of the killing. On the underground station this may involve firstly selecting the victim, and then, as the train comes in, separating him from his companions; holding him back from the train for just enough time for the theft to occur; and finally changing tack and positively easing him onto the train to speed off penniless towards his destination.

All of this has to be managed without any sort of gross movement which might draw attention to what's happening. Geoff, as a professional stall, had nothing but contempt for the snatchers and jostlers and muggers. They were 'hooligans' or 'cowboys' or 'gas-meter bandits'. His game was to use his entire body to keep the victim in such a position that the hook could work inside his pocket without making any tell-tale contact with the sides. And all the blocking and checking movements carried out with back and hands and feet had to be disguised as natural ones – as what anyone might do as he was trying to board a train, or readjust a raincoat over his arm, or read the cartoon on page four of the *Standard*.

It was the gradual public switch to 'plastic money' – to credit cards – which moved Geoff on from pickpocketing and towards his present trade. Ironically enough in the early days – the 1950s and even the 1960s – credit cards were simply dumped along with the wallet. But then the opportunities began to be realized. Credit cards became valuable.

'Give me a credit card, Laurie. See this American Express.' Geoff held up my card. 'See this stuff you've got on it here.' He pointed to the patterned strip behind the signature. 'Now as soon as you interfere with that, it comes off and leaves a mark. Right? Have you got any more cards there, Laurie?' I got out my little concertina pack and Geoff selected the Barclaycard.

'On Barclays now, they've got a "VOID" behind it. You see?' He pointed at the signature strip on the card. 'Behind there. All this'd come up "VOID" if you try to take the signature off. But a few years ago it was just a plain bit of white. Nothing behind it.'

I was beginning to relax a little. I was close enough to the cassette-recorder to see the central reels slowly turning and know that all was well there: John hadn't shot me a McVigour look for ages: some of the embarassment I'd accumulated in my head in the last few days began to melt away. The best news of all was the sheer momentum of Geoff's speech. No need to think of the next question for a moment or two. I allowed myself the luxury of watching for a moment and let Panasonic do the listening.

Geoff had a staccato style: machine-gun bursts of words, punctuated with chopping hand movements, and a favourite phrase 'Boom–boom–boom', very rapidly delivered, to cover any period of time in which a piece of action unfolded as it was meant to: in which a scheme went exactly as planned. 'So down we went. Boom–boom–boom. On the train. Shaped up this wallie. Boom–boom–boom. We hadn't been working for ten minutes. By the door. Boom–boom–boom. And then he's going, "Oh dear, look what's happened. That man over there." And I'm going, "This way?" and that, trying to help. "Which way'd they go?" *Two grand*.

But even though I often got lost by the story, I rarely missed the point, for Geoff was a bit like an old-time fourth-form teacher, always checking the faces around him for signs of comprehension, for evidence that they'd got his meaning. And alongside that was the mime, his ability to act out scenes from his story, often using the entire room for a stage, without a break in the narrative.

'But didn't the bleach mess up the rest of the card?' John asked. I stopped watching Geoff's style and hooked myself back to the story of how to recycle Barclaycards.

'No, no. You'd seal this gold part up.' He pointed to the bottom third of the card. 'Used to be black in those days – never used to be gold – so that the black never came off – with sellotape and all that. And bleach it. Take it out and rinse it off. Then we'd just tape it up again, seal it off with sellotape right round the signature space. Perfect, you know. Then you buy that white spray. Aerosol. Just give it a couple of whooshes.' His hand swept backwards and forwards across the card. 'It was perfect. Brand new card. Blank. Put your own writing on it. No need to copy anything.'

It certainly sounded simple enough, and even though Geoff was no longer stealing the cards himself, his part ownership of a club in the West End meant that he had had his own little clearing-house for credit cards which had been nicked by burglars and hotel workers. What brought this game to an end was not so much the introduction of the VOID sign behind the signature space, but the problems which built up when people used their own handwriting for the signatures on the renovated cards. 'The handwriting was traced, wasn't it? It builds up as you work. It's all computerized, and the more that writing goes out . . . I mean you can disguise it so it looks different, which they did try and do in the end . . . but in those days there was a lot of people using their ordinary writing, and what they got was a build-up of all the different wroughts.' [Wroughts were dramatic situations or scenes.]

'You know what I mean?' Geoff was quick enough to spot some incomprehension, although not its exact source. 'Bad blues. Nowadays, anyone who knows what they're doing would rather copy a signature. Once you copy someone else's monicker, there's no evidence of the handwriting.'

People may think that they can produce a signature which is unrecognizable as their own, but of course they're going to have to repeat this in front of a shopkeeper or a teller, so however hard they try to dissimulate, there's likely to be quite enough left in the formation of vowels and consonants for some sort of record to build up. And it's just that cumulative aspect which goes straight to the heart of the difference between the professional and the amateur thief.

Con men like Geoff are not just concerned with successfully bringing off today's crime. They're also watching the risks of long-term detection. This is not one job for them. This is going to work for a long period of time – maybe years, and so it's essential that no single crime can possibly lead to the detection of any others, One offence with a Barclaycard is a fine, 350 revealed by computer comparison could be ten years. 'Only an amateur', Geoff insisted, 'would now use his own handwriting. Anyone who knows what he's doing would make sure and copy someone else's signature.'

There's a Thurber cartoon which shows a couple of guests at a party standing talking to each other while over to the right of them a completely naked lady is shown playing energetically at a piano. 'I'd feel much easier about it if her husband hadn't gone to bed,' runs the caption. A variation on the cartoon flashed into my head when a glance to my left revealed that while Geoff was elaborating upon the detailed skills of the professional credit-card forger and other such routine villainy, his wife had been quietly unpacking a shopping bag on the Heals table at the far end of the room. Was it that nobody except me had spotted her, or was there a tacit agreement between Geoff and John that they wouldn't notice? How much were wives expected to know about the professional criminal careers of their husbands? Perhaps John would know: I remember he'd had a wife. At least, he had in the film.

Meanwhile, Geoff was taking another angle on forgery – on what was worth forging and what was not. 'And I'll tell you something else, John – never handle forged gear.' I could tell from Geoff's mime of a bank-clerk flicking through a wad that we were talking of forged banknotes. 'No one handles forgery, only fools. Anyone who handles forged gear gets into trouble. I swear to you.'

'But I suppose you must get some good forgeries,' I said. 'You know, ones you can't tell from the real thing.'

'It's the biggest load of crap in the world,' Geoff insisted. 'It's all mythical. All that garbage in the papers about it being the real way to make money. All you're working for is the printers – the people that make it. I've been offered loads of stuff – forged traveller's cheques, forged dollars. Not interested. You get nothing out of it.' He carefully chose the definitive phrase with which to dismiss it: 'It's a bad blue. There's a terrible scream with it.'

'It's all sheer profit though, isn't it?' I was reluctant to abandon a recurrent dream of my own printing-press on which I'd simply run off another few hundred five-pound notes whenever the time came to trade in the Datsun.

'Not at all. Suppose you can buy American dollars for a third. [Geoff's fractions – halves, thirds, quarters – always related to the face value of the commodity.] 'Hundred-dollar bills say. Or say five-hundred-dollar bills. Whatever the case. You go to the bank. You could just go in a bank and change 'em.' The absence of Geoff's usual 'Boom–boom–boom' to indicate the routine nature of the job suggested that trouble lay ahead.

'Now, they've got to be perfect dollars . . . they know the little things to look for. And they never are perfect. Forged stuff. And I've seen some pretty good ones. Right?'

John gave him the nod he wanted.

'Right. So you change up. Top wack. Five hundred dollars. You can't do more than that. Anything over that and they're gonna go away.' A quick half-circular twist of his index finger stood for the teller going back behind the glass to check the lists.

'They always know there's a lot of forged around. Especially dollars. Even in American banks they won't change it. Credit cards they want. They don't want dollars. Or any other money. Not in a bank.' Nothing about the tone of his final clinching statement on the subject suggested any ironic intent. '*Money is the worst thing in the world to walk into a bank with.*'

'I mean, suppose you do change up five hundred dollars. Right? They stand you in a third, don't they? So you've earned what? You've earned about ... ninety quid ... whatever the exchange rate might be. But now you've got to go to another bank and do it again.'

And that didn't mean just walking in. Getting yourself ready for encounters like this was a strain. Something could always go wrong: you were increasing the risk all the time. I heard later from a store detective about the number of professional hoisters (shop-lifters) he'd found sitting exhausted on the emergency staircases which ran down the side of the shop – not hiding, but recuperating: gathering up their psychological resources and their facial mannerisms, accents, posture, ready for the next encounter. They needed to let their front fall away in the wings so that they could assume it properly when they walked back onto the stage. And with dollar bills to change, you were firmly in the limelight.

'Each transaction takes a quarter of an hour at the foreign counter. Standing in front of the glass. They've got your boat [boat – boatrace – face], dabs ... everything. All aggravation. No dough in it. And if you get nicked with it – it's the crime of the century. You get seven or eight [years]. Millions of mugs go out with it and get in trouble with it.'

So what was the medium to work with, the one which gave the least aggravation? Geoff had no doubt at all. He'd now reached the happy stage where he doubted if commercial practice could improve upon the medium of exchange which was the stuff of his existence – TCs, traveller's cheques. 'With TCs, John, they don't remember you. In and out. One boat among a thousand. You work clean and get just as much money. With no big blues. And if you get nicked with a few TCs buzzed [stolen] out of a hotel, well, it's not the end of the world, is it?'

To tell the truth, I was rather embarassed by Geoff's description of how he played the criminal law, his careful calculation of the likely sentence for this or that offence, and then the decision to lay off those like forgery which might get you a 'seven' or 'eight'. Over the years I'd given countless lectures on the need to reduce prison sentences. I'd carefully outline the research which showed that long sentences were no more effective than short ones in deterring potential offenders, then turn to the Dutch experience, pass round a few histograms, and finish with a quotation from Churchill about a country's penal policy being the most accurate guide to its state of civilization.

All admirably liberal, and usually well received. Unfortunately, none of it fitted the present indication from Geoff that the early introduction of a statutory sentence of ten years for handling stolen traveller's cheques would do much to eliminate the offence most favoured by professional fraudsters.

But, if likely sentence was so very critical, why had Geoff abandoned cheque book and cards? The risk involved in presenting a traveller's cheque and a dodgy passport seemed, if anything, greater than using a cheque and card, and yet sentences were similar. I was keen enough on my penal policy to press the point.

'Well, it was stamina, wasn't it?'

'Stamina?'

'Yes stamina. We used to go out with book and card. Right? But it's only fifty quid a time. Right? Fifty quid. Fifty quid. Fifty quid.' Geoff imitated the poker player dealing three hands of five-pound notes.

Fifty quid a time certainly sounded OK, but as he'd have gone 'half-way' on the deal with the original thief, it was only twenty-five for each successful transaction. Not that there was any shortage of these. Geoff's voice and pace rose to accommodate the vividness of his memories.

'I'll tell you. We used to go down the road. Get out of the car. And there might be a street of banks. Lloyds, Barclays, Midland, National Westminster – a whole street. And we all had crooked books and cards. It was a joke at first. We used to call a street of banks a milk run. We planned it so that we could have special runs down streets where there was no traffic and we could get most banks in. The record – the all-time record for anyone – was 53 in one day. Fifty-three banks in one day. Half-past nine to half-past three. It was like going down the Underground again. Sometimes there'd be three of us in the same bank together. All with crooked gear.'

John was laughing by now. At the sheer excess. All those banks and tellers; all the times that Geoff had to get out of the car; in a terrible hurry to try to beat the record; putting on yet another casual pose before strolling in and hoping to find an available teller. And the absurdity of being locked into a competition to see who could cheat the biggest number of banks in a single day. That record of 53. Imagine going into a bank even five times in one day. But 53! Geoff waited a second for John's laughter to clear, and then with professional timing piled on the agony.

'If I tell you . . . listen, John. I used to get so much money, so much, that in the end I started to cheat. *I started to cheat.* Instead of doing all the book, I'd tear out half and pay for it with my own money. Right?'

No, it wasn't quite right, I couldn't understand; even though it meant putting a stopper into Geoff's effervescence. He went round again to clear my puzzlement. *'I'd tear out half the book and pay for it with my own money*. When it came to the end of the day and we were reckoning up, I'd put some money up out of my own pocket and make out I'd changed up cheques I hadn't.' The need to explain it so carefully made the irony a little more evident. 'Oh well, I suppose it wasn't exactly my money, but you know what I mean.'

Off to my left I could see that Geoff's wife was now watering the houseplants on the Waring and Gillow bookcase. Her face suggested that none of the excitement or laughter which was now running freely at our end of the room had touched her directly.

Geoff was in any case already far too caught up by the further intricacies of 'book and card' to notice anything else around him. 'You see, you must never go into a Barclays with a Barclay. Always go into a National with a Barclay. And a Lloyds with a Midland. Right?'

The ashtray in front of us was picked up and emptied into the fireplace and returned. 'My wife'd tell you,' announced Geoff. A witness had arrived on cue. 'I used to wake up in my sleep shouting out "ten fives" "ten fives". See, I always asked for ten fives in every bank. And it got so bad I used to have nightmares about it. It was in my head so much. I used to say to her, "Gwen they're driving me mad." Didn't I?' The witness nodded. Geoff turned back to us. Witness dismissed. Matters became entirely personal again. 'I don't know whether I'm coming or going. Right? *Don't go in a Barclays with a Barclay. Don't go in a National with a Nat.* I couldn't handle it. I couldn't handle it.'

Many of the other 'lives of crime' that I was to come across had just this thread of routine villainy running through them. Far too much emphasis gets placed on major professional crimes; the big con which nets £2 million, the bullion raid which pulls in £12 million, the successful theft of £5 million worth of jewellery. What makes such crimes possible is the existence of a whole network of lesser crimes which sustain professional criminals throughout the rest of the year. It isn't a case of two kinds of professional criminals – the small-time and the big-time. Only the opportunities which are available fit into these two categories. The criminals move between them. Whenever the police were successful in cracking major cases (usually by a complicated system of deals and counter-deals), the villains turned out to be well known to the people I was interviewing. There was no surprise.

'I see "Manchester Tony" was on that Guildford job.'

'Oh yes, he's been at it for years.'

This had just been a big break, the big job which had come someone's way as a result of all the everyday 'ducking and diving': news of a gullible Arab, the discovery of a pliable security guard; inside knowledge from hotel room-service.

But as Geoff had found with the 'book and card' routine, some of the routine villainy could start to feel awfully like work, and that was the time to move on. Particularly if the con was getting harder. And that was just the position with book and card.

'Give me your cheque book, Laurie.' Geoff now had all my credit cards and cheque book on the table in front of him. 'Now look at the back page. Right? Where it says, "This Page for Bank Use Only." Now they've perfected that, made it hard.'

Initially, Geoff explained, the 'Bank Use Only' page was put there merely to keep customers on the rails and to stop them popping in for a second £50 (or £30 as it was in those days) before the bank had a chance to check their balance. So originally it was just a sticky label which the teller stamped with the date. This might have deterred the average punter who was trying to slip in two bank visits a day, but it was easy meat for anyone with a routine milk run of banks to cover before 3.30.

'Well, of course, we went and had them printed up. Got our own labels printed. But ours had different glue on them.

So that they didn't used to stick for long: they just used to be tacky and stay on for ...' (Geoff hesitated, the period was too short for measurement) '... you just peel it off after each draw and put on another one. And then go in the next bank.'

Those relatively easy times lasted a year. You didn't have to do too much printing because the labels didn't have the customer's name on them. So you might use up 30 or 40 on one day – taking one off and replacing it with another after each transaction; and, of course, you could start again with the same labels on the day afterwards. Just so long as you never used a label which showed the same date twice.

Then the banks got together. Lloyds, Barclays and Nat. West. "*Item six on the agenda: Geoff*. Any suggestions as to what we might do about this consummate villain and his friends who are swindling us out of thousands a week by getting their own sticky labels printed and substituting them for ours? Yes, Corbishley – it is Corbishley isn't it? Let's hear your plan.'

It was predictable, but clever enough to be going on with. Instead of sticky labels, they used the actual cheque book. Put squares all over the inside of the back cover.

So one morning – and it was as sudden as that – Geoff and his friends woke up with a major threat to their employment. And some useless sticky labels.

'You just had to have the back of the book. No other way. So now I went to the printers and had the backs made. So we could change the backs.'

This meant, of course, that Geoff had to rebind the cheque book between visits to the bank so that today's date was never marked on the back squares. So, the black sticky binding would be loosened in the cheque book, as well as the two bits of wire which stapled the cheques together.

'But it was aggravation, cos you had to do it secretly in the car or the cab. Back of the cab. Right? And you might be trying to work quick and it slowed things down a bit. Cos each time you'd go in, the book's got a different back on it. But you can use the whole back up. You didn't have to have many printed. And they looked better as they filled up. As you went along. But sometimes they got in such a mess you couldn't use them any more. The binding got all tacky and wouldn't stick down at all, so you were going in with it all falling out and the wire sticking through. I thought, this is no good.'

It looked like game, set and match to Corbishley. But Geoff had found yet another card to play. He picked up my cheque book again. At the far end of the room his wife had started to lay the table for the children's tea. Scones. Bread and butter.

'Suddenly I realized that every bank does a *small* cheque book. Not a big one like this. One with no stubs in it. All you've got left after the cheques are used is an empty cover with that set of squares for stamping printed on it. Marvellous really. So all you had to do was collect up a few of these covers off the small books and then you'd put one cheque in the back. As though it was the last one. You'd go in, sling it over, and they'd just take your last cheque and stamp the back wouldn't they. No wires, no tacky binding. Boom–boom–boom. And off you went on the milk run once again – only this time with a pocket of empty cheque books – and a wad of "last cheques".'

They must have called another meeting of major banks. ('Well, gentlemen, any other suggestions? No, not you Corbishley.') And this time they found the real solution. The idea of using the cover was abandoned and instead the 'Bank Use Only' page became an integral part of the book itself, with the customer's name and account number and bank code overprinted on the front side, just as on a cheque. It wasn't the problem of printing these pages which deterred Geoff; that could still be handled, and the pages slipped in at the end as you went from bank to bank. It was the time this extra work required.

'To get a printer to do these overnight is very difficult. Especially as you can't keep them. They've got to go down (be used) the next day or the day after. So, top wack, you might have two days to get that printed with the number and name on it and all that business. So I looked for an easier wrought.'

He found it in traveller's cheques. But although this was a similar game to 'book and card' in terms of likely sentence for being found in possession, and although like 'book and card' it also involved strolling into a bank and signing a signature which wasn't yours, it did have one great advantage for Geoff. It wasn't routine. It demanded skill – his particular skill.

'It isn't like going to an ordinary window in a jug [bank] and saying "Er, £50 please. Ten fives." And then, sweet as a nut, the bird behind the counter slings it over. Boom–boom–boom. Stamps the book. "There you are, Sir." Readies. Right? With TCs it's different. It's big chunks of money and it's not straightforward. You have to go round to the foreign counter. And they used to dwell on it. "Look at this. Look at that." It's much more ... it needs much more finesse ... much more personal ... *much more of a con.*'

3

THE BEAUTY OF A GOOD CON

*In which John becomes edgy – a giant piranha expires – the
value of distraction becomes clear – and the author learns where
the Queen goes in Oxford Street.*

I had an idea his pride was hurt when I said I'd make my
own way over to the Horse and Groom this Sunday
lunchtime. But I hadn't quite expected such crude revenge.
And there was no other word for what was going on. My
speedometer made it absolutely clear.

Every time we came towards green traffic lights, me and
my Datsun Violet about 30 or 40 yards behind John's Escort
TIX, I'd notice that his speed dipped slightly, say back from
45 to 40-ish, and simultaneously I'd spot the slight movement
in his left shoulder which indicated that he was changing
down rather than letting me see any tell-tale brake-lights.
Then, if the lights stayed at green, up would go the speed
again as we raced through them. But if they went to amber he
would stay dawdling at 30-ish for another couple of seconds,
and then, vroom-vroom through, leaving me with the option
of going over a red or losing him entirely.

Maybe I'd have been less alert to the dodge if he hadn't been
telling me only the week before about an opposite ploy –
about how as an armed robber, you had to spend a lot of time
stealing cars and moving them around. Not only getting cars
to take you to the bank, but arranging a series of change cars
for the getaway. When stolen cars were on the move, they
needed to be 'back-and-fronted' by straight cars in a three car
convoy to shield them from police attention. And that meant
never towing anyone through an amber or red.

Round the corner into Russell Square from Southampton

Row. Greens all the way. Down towards Senate House. London University. The car-park where they put up the finals results. Those top windows in the tower which were supposed to be narrower than the lower ones to enhance the sense of height. In fact, one of my classmates at Birkbeck had based a short poem on the illusion – 'False Perspectives', no less – about how higher education failed to give you any proper sense of brute reality.

> Curiously.
> Those peering from their ivory windows
> Lack height and vision
> Simultaneously.
> Such is the illusion's strength.

Rather sad really. There he was, lecturing in cognitive psychology at a West Country university, while I was racing through red lights round the back of my Alma Mater in pursuit of an armed robber who seemed determined to get me killed or arrested.

I was beginning to think it wasn't just my insistence on using my own car that he was sulking about. A few red lights would have made that point. But now he was still at it as we crossed the Euston Road. There was another likely cause. We'd had a disagreement after getting back from Geoff's flat. All I'd been doing was trying out aloud a few headings for writing up the project. Perhaps, I'd suggested, a section on Geoff's self-deceptions: his need to believe that his trickery wasn't hurting anyone else, and how this contrasted with his view of most humanity as 'straights' or 'wallies'; his idea that he'd eventually make enough money to get out of the game altogether, but at the same time his obsession with gambling and the high life.

At first John had said nothing. I'd presumed he was vaguely admiring my ideas, perhaps thinking of other paradoxes which would fill out this section on con men and their values.

'Perhaps we could do a bit of writing tomorrow morning,' I'd gone on breezily. Overlooking the long silence.

'Yeah,' he managed. 'I'll see ya then.' For someone who treated my precisest arrangements as chord structures around which to improvise, that meant 'Forget it.' At least it gave me a free morning to get the bibliography in some sort of order.

We were nearly there. And what's more, the lights were now finally on my side. Every set on the long run down Euston Road had such an incorruptible greenness about them that even John gave up trying to precipitate changes by approaching them with mock temerity.

At least Geoff was friendly. 'Laurie. Good to see you. Here,' tipping Sancerre into a free glass. 'You like this dry white don't you?' I was to become less flattered by this sensitivity to the taste of others when I learnt to recognize it as part of the trading culture of spielers and drinking clubs: 'Here Mick, you like cashmere don't you?' was a favourite cue for some earnest chatter and eventually for a couple of car-boots to be backed close together outside.

'Cheers!'

The bar was much more crowded than the previous Sunday. There even seemed to be a musical trio in the far corner of the room battling it out against what sounded like Marvin Gaye on the speakers. 'Mostly thieves,' John said when I looked at him for a clue.

Les was nowhere in sight. 'Probably dealing with more wroughts over the aquaria,' said Geoff.

It was the first news I heard of a saga which was to rumble its way throughout the project. The tropical fish con. As far as I could ever tell, it had all started out as a viable commercial project. Another of those ways of saying goodbye to a life of crime which periodically poke their seductive peaks above the foothills of daily villainy. Someone – a friend of Les's, I think – had actually invented an aquarium which was ideal for the reception areas and foyers of large commercial organizations. It was very large (someone mentioned 30 gallons of water, but that may have been a Beano figure invented more in the service of humour than accuracy) and it incorporated such advanced food-delivering and self-cleaning functions that it only required servicing every couple of months. What could be more attractive? Although the hire fee was admittedly rather high – £200 a month – your customers and visitors were guaranteed the permanent sight of multi-coloured tropical fish swimming contentedly around their self-sufficient tank.

There was only one snag: a small matter which made the aquarium a 'conning' proposition rather than a commercial one. The dull scientific truth was that, although the tanks did deliver appropriate amounts of food at regular intervals and did indeed clean themselves through a complicated network of inter-locking filters, the electrical system was quite unable to provide simultaneously the temperate conditions which were essential to the survival of your actual tropical fish.

Les was undeterred. Round he went to offices, banks and estate agents, and cheerfully signed up a long list of eager punters. And into foyers and reception areas and directorial suites went the magnificent tanks stocked to the brim, not with brightly coloured swordtails, platys, tetras, loaches and plecs, but with (what Les affectionately called) 'little black-and-grey buggers' who could live anywhere.

Not surprisingly, the phone started to ring after a couple of weeks.

'Ah. Excuse me. I'm so sorry to bother you. But it's about the aquarium.'

'That's a very good aquarium.'

'Yes, yes. I'm certain it is. In fact, no complaints on that score. But it's just the fish.'

'Yes?'

'Well, I thought you said we'd be getting tropical fish.'

'Yes.'

'Well, the one's we've got seem to be all black and grey.'

Les would then get very stroppy indeed. 'Don't be silly,' he'd go. 'Don't be so ignorant. What you've got there are *very young* tropical fish. They develop all their colours as they get older.'

It was quite plausible enough to spin out the con for six or seven months, and now, at least a year later, the story was still as fresh as ever. Something about the vision of hundreds of chief executives bundling into work every morning and peering through the glass of the tank, in the hope of detecting some golden threads among the grey, was quite enough to send hysteria rippling through the average crowd of London villains.

And this Sunday Geoff was bringing John up to date on another episode in the long-running farce. It seemed that in the early days of the scheme, he'd decided to give Les a hand with one of the more bizarre promotion ideas for the aquaria – a special stand at the Ideal Home Exhibition. Off he went on the story. I was delighted. Goodness knows what it had to say about the values of the professional criminal, but nothing was better calculated to get John back into the frame of mind where I could switch on the cassette without him going all McVigour over me.

'So we wanted a piranha, didn't we. But we had to get the biggest piranha there was. Right? So we go round to this guy who runs a big fish place near Shepherd's Bush. Big trade in piranhas. And listen, John, you'll like this. D'you know who buys them from him? His best customers? *Screws!*' Then for my benefit: 'Prison screws. They love 'em. Can't get enough. Take them home to their little brick houses behind Wandsworth nick and sit and throw mice at them. Now this man knew where the biggest piranha was. A mate of his had got it. Enormous fucker. Huge mouth. Like this. And that's all. No body.' Geoff's hands outlined the shape of this mutant. 'But he didn't want us to have it. "I've been breeding piranhas for years and this is the best." All that. All this and that. So we pay him a lump to hire this fish. This big fucking mouth. And off to the Ideal Home. But you see, what we don't know is this. You can't put a piranha in a big tank. No, you can't John. At least not a tank as dodgy as the one we had. Because when it gets mad it's got more room to get up speed and then it can zap across the water like . . .' Geoff imitated its speed and trajectory with a flattened hand, 'and smash straight through the glass. So you have to put it in a little tank where it can't turn round and get a run. But we're selling big tanks. Les has this bright idea. We'll get a little tank which'll just fit around the piranha and put it in the Press Club with a notice saying "Biggest Fucking Piranha in the World" – and then all stuff about our wonderful aquaria being on stand So-and-So.

'So we got the little tank, stuffed the piranha in, and put it on a shelf in the Press Club. Two hundred and fifty quid piranha. Right? Three days later. I'll tell you John, you're not going to believe this.' Geoff's premonitions of John's incredulity were not prompted in any way by John: they were dramatic pauses which helped him to milk more laughter from his audience. 'As true as I stand here, John. In I go. Into the Press Club. *Incredible*! *Incredible*! Those reporters have seen "Piranha" on the side and they've been throwing stuff into the tank for it to eat. Really, John. Everything's in there. You wouldn't believe it. Peanuts, crisps, half a sandwich, even a fucking beefburger. Everything. And there's this daft piranha buried underneath it all. Buried. Two hundred and fifty quid's worth. This fella's prize piranha. Fucking hell!'

Later, in the Landsdowne, I was to hear the equally true story of how the main display tank began to leak at the

Ideal Home Exhibition and gradually submerged the neighbouring stands. And then, from Michael, one night at the Jacaranda, about the Italian restaurant in Maida Vale which still has one of the faulty tanks perched high above a table where loving couples nightly dine in happy ignorance of the floodtide which might at any moment sweep them and their *Pollo Sorpresa* out into the Edgware Road.

Although the joke mainly rested on the idea of sophisticated men about town – Les and Geoff – trying to come to terms with the requirements of such absurd creatures as fish, the loudest laughter was reserved for those wallies who actually hired the tanks, or spent time breeding piranhas, or simply liked looking at fish swimming about. After all, it was the discomfiture of these straights which provided such solid confirmation that only proper villains were 'in the know'.

But even if the world outside was filled with wallies – people forever ready to believe what they read in the paper or saw on the television – there was still a distinction to be made between, say, wallies and proper wallies. In fact, Geoff's fame as a stall rested precisely upon his ability to make that distinction. He was always first into the bank so that he could quickly 'clock' the tellers and subtly direct his accomplice towards the right counter. He'd mentioned this at the flat, but only as we'd been leaving, and I'd been unable to pursue it. But now, even with Tamla still driving hard through the speakers, the optics taking a heavy hammering, and the air thick enough with the smell of marijuana to poleaxe a tracker dog, I decided to go for details. I let the aquarium hysteria around me wash away, sipped a little more Sancerre, and switched on the cassette. John chose to ignore it.

'Geoff, when you're doing one of those bank jobs . . .' – sometimes my attempts at the vernacular embarrassed me a good two seconds before they hit John – 'how do you know which of the tellers to pick?' In this thick, diffuse atmosphere, the bald question rattled like a table-tennis ball, but Geoff, having scored with his piranha, obviously decided that he could spare a few sprats for me.

'Cos you can tell by the faces. You can see a teller and say, "Shitt Nitto." Cos you know by the boat. Understand? And you can see a kind face – or you can see an idiot. But you can see 'em. And once you'd got the right teller, you stayed with 'em.'

'I had this girl once. In a Lloyds bank in the West End. We used to wait for her. If she wasn't there, we used to walk out and wait for her to come in. Oh, we kept doing her with TCs. We'd go along there one day – listen John, this girl was amazing – and I'd say to my partner Bimbo (who's doing the signing), "She ain't in Bim. Must be at lunch." Anyway, she's right down this road, this busy road near Euston Station. And she's seen us on the pavement. "Sir," she shouts to Bim, and runs down the road. "Are you waiting for me? I won't be a minute." And she's rushed in and got behind her thing and opened the drawer for him. Five-hundred-dollar cheque. A big lump.'

The accuracy of Geoff's character assessment is quite enough to give him a higher status than Bimbo (or any other accomplice) whose job it is to sign the traveller's cheques and manage the accent which goes with the nationality they betray. Bimbo had been 'at the dip' – pickpocketing – when he'd come to Geoff and begged for a chance to work with him. Now he'd developed into a key man.

'He's top class. He can be anything. He can be an old man. He can be thirty-five or sixty. He can be any accent, German, Italian or French. Anything. If I tell you . . .' – he laughed at the memory. 'This bird we kept doing. Well, Bimbo's in the bank and we've already done her a few times. Not too much. Three or four hundred quid. All of a sudden there's an Indian customer shouting and waving his arms at the manager. We're in the queue at this bird's till. Now Bimbo's gone over and said to the Indian in his broad American: "See, leave that man alone. How dare you." And the manager's scuttled back behind the thing. "Thank you very much, sir," he's saying to Bim. The bird's looking at Bim and says "Oh sir, you shouldn't have. Thanks *ever* so much." Oh we had her, this bird, for months after that.'

If these lucky opportunities to gain credibility don't come along, life is more difficult. Tellers will go and look at lists when there's an unfamiliar face cashing big cheques. Some may be gullible, but it's rare to find a complete wally. So much so that Geoff recalled the one and only incident with absolute delight.

'I found this geezer in a Barclays bank. No, it was another Lloyds. No, Barclays.' (I remembered that getting the bank right was important in Geoff's trade.) 'This fellow looked as if he'd come out of a nuthouse.' Geoff was exultant. 'Honest. His hair was all clipped. 'I'm not exaggerating. And he had pimples everywhere. Amazing. You know those poor things you see in mental homes that have really gone. One of those. In a fucking bank. Would you believe it?

'Well we went to him with traveller's cheques for two months. I'm telling you, it got bigger and bigger. Two-thousand-dollar cheques. Nine hundred quid over the counter. And in the end . . . in the end . . . he ran out of money in his till. You won't believe it, John.' John was whooping with laughter. 'And he was going along all the other tills taking money out and giving them chits for it.'

I was laughing along with John – if a little less grossly – I mean, perhaps the man was on some sort of mental hospital release scheme – it wasn't that funny. Geoff spotted that some liberal sensibilities were getting in the way of his audience appreciation. 'Oh yeah, Laurie,' he said, eyeing me hard, as though he was dealing with a point of information from the floor. 'That's how we work. Just find a nice kind face and *slaughter* them.'

But I'd also been a bit reserved in my laughter because I couldn't help spotting a fatal flaw in all these stories. Surely, there was no point in finding a gullible teller, even one who looked as if he'd just come out of a nuthouse, because when the bank found out that any of the cheques you'd passed were phoney, the tellers would be on the lookout for you. Ready to give the manager the nod and a wink when you next appeared. However stupid they were. However much of a wally.

'No, that's it, Laurie. That's the secret, I know. I know,' and he went slowly and quietly to allow me to give his knowledge proper weight: 'I know – they ... can't ... tell ... these ... tellers. I know in my heart that they couldn't tell 'em. They don't call them in a week after we've hit 'em and say: "Look, you took these stolen traveller's cheques, the other day" – Boom–Boom–Boom.' Geoff laid them out on the manager's desk before the fictional embarrassed teller: "Now, who was it?" They don't say nothing, see. Not a word. You see if they did, they'd have a paranoid staff, wouldn't they? Always looking suspicious and staring at every customer. They can't do it. The staff couldn't handle it. Ordinary people getting sixty quid a week seeing every customer as a terrible villian? Can you imagine what it'd do to business? They couldn't handle it.'

It was only convincing when you thought about it for a moment: thought of the sheer number of transactions in a single day; the impossibility of running a careful check on more than a small proportion; the danger of alienating genuine customers by appearing the least bit suspicious. And anyway, Geoff had a clincher which he'd been saving: 'Cos if they knew, they might also get an idea to slip their own people in to do it. They might say: "Cor, if you get the TCs, I'm behind the ramp." "Yeah, I'll do that – that's easy." *So they don't tell them.*'

So much professional crime relies on just this sort of

exploitation of the unpatrolled moments of social life: those occasions when banks, security firms, department stores, bookmakers, bullion dealers and credit companies leave the door just a little bit ajar because the invitation it offers to customers is felt to outweigh the opportunity it offers to villains.

But although this principle of trust meant that Geoff and his accomplices could usually find a teller without any preconceived suspicions, it did nothing to ensure that suspicions wouldn't be aroused during the actual transaction. There were so many potential mistakes. On the previous Wednesday, I'd gone through the routine myself – cashing a cheque in my local Lloyds and imagining that it was phoney. Did I usually say 'Morning' when I got to the grille? It sounded very strange today. What did I write first on the cheque? The date? 'Pay cash'? The amount? And most important – because remember I was about to copy someone else's signature – when could I reasonably take out the cheque card which contained the signature I had to match? Didn't I usually write the cheque and then take out the card? And then, at what precise second did I say 'Ten fives'. As she stamped the cheque? Or marked the book? Or did I wait for her face to give that slight, questioning lift?

This simple scene is Geoff's permanent occupational drama. He has played it in thousands of banks throughout the United Kingdom. 'Ah Scotland,' he'd say, 'Now they are real banks. Do you know, John, they'd never give you dirty notes in a Scottish bank. They wouldn't, John. You get respect in a Scottish bank.' He knew Italian and French and Scandinavian and even Australian banks. 'Australia's the place John. I'll tell you. They know nothing there. They're babies. Just waiting to be taken.' (This wasn't just wanderlust on Geoff's part. Traveller's cheques were international. And if someone managed to nick a big pile of them in England, it made sense sometimes to move quickly to some other country like Spain, where they were notoriously slow at circulating news of such losses.)

And wherever the scene was played, a key element was likely to be the *distraction*. You could get all the opening pleasantries exactly right, have all the initial moves synchronized like clockwork, but then there was the actual signing to manage. Anything beyond four seconds can begin to look like strange even to a foreign teller just out of a nuthouse. More than seven seconds is a give-away. Try it for yourself. You can almost feel the touch of the manager's hand on your shoulder as that seventh second creeps up. In the circumstances, anything which can give the signer a bonus couple of seconds is vital. And Geoff's distractions are tailored to do just that.

The routine varies depending on the circumstances, the length of queues at the tills, the amount of extra time needed to get a particular 'monicker' right. The 'diary' is an old favourite. As Bimbo bends to the signing, Geoff's head suddenly pops in front of the teller's line of vision: 'Oh excuse me. I'm so sorry. But did I leave my diary in here yesterday?' (Four seconds.) Or perhaps the Queen Mother routine. This one is directed at those who are standing next to him in a neighbouring queue, but pitched just high enough for the teller's ears: 'Such a shame about the Queen Mother. Still she made 80 and she's been a wonderful lady.' General consternation. (Say three seconds.)

With all the free time I'd had during the week, while John was away somewhere in Notting Hill doing anything but turning up in Battersea to go through the synopsis, I'd had time to read up on other famous con men. One of the most famous of all time was an American, nicknamed 'Christmas' Parmelee because of his preference for working banks during the Christmas rush. I'd relished his 'distracting' line enough to ask Geoff if he'd like to hear it.

'Yeah, go on Laurie.'

'Well, apparently, he'd be just signing the cheque, and then he'd look up at the teller and go: "Oh, I say. I wonder can I trouble you for half a dozen rubber bands? The manager said you might have some."

A gem. I could see Geoff thought so too. It not only distracted, but gave credibility by suggesting that old Parmelee had just been having a chin-wag with the manager himself. An almost magical phrase really when measured by the golden eggs it produced over the years. The 'abracadabra' – the wave of the wand in the right hand – which lets the left get quickly on with the real business.

Not that Geoff was ready to get carried away by my metaphors. After all that funny-funny distraction, there was still the very serious business of making certain that the successfully signed cheque was now cashed. Tellers will often make a routine check on the customer, have a look at their list of suspect names and numbers behind the counter. If Bimbo ran away every time that happened, there'd be few pay-days for Geoff and him. His job is to stand there casually and wait while Geoff from his position at the back of the queue makes an assessment of the dangers involved in the teller's every move. It was getting hard to catch his words as the speakers in the Horse and Groom piled on a few more decibels for 'I Heard it through the Grapevine', but I cranked the cassette recording-level deep into the red section and hoped for the best.

'Now, if she's walking away with the gear, I'll walk right along the counter and find out where she is. Look at her. Right? She might be looking at old lists. She might be on the blower. I can tell if it's trouble.' He stared hard at John to emphasize the point. 'I know by the boat. The boat always gives them away. And if the cheque's off, they can't handle it by themselves. That's the clue. They've got to look for help. And they're shaking. They're always shaking. They go to the manager – "Blah, blah, blah". Geoff dramatized the nervous *sotto voce* conversation for us. 'But before we get to that, *I've* got it. I've given the sign and Bimbo's straight out of the jug. Right? You see John, you've always got time. Only seconds. But you've got time. Provided . . . provided you're looking at everything.'

And, of course, Geoff's main advantage in the situation is that nobody connects him in any way with the attempted fraud. He's just another customer. In his words: 'I'm not in on the wrought. I'm there dwelling up; changing up some money. Nobody sniffs me out as the other guy.'

Only once or twice had it gone really wrong. And then Geoff as the innocent bystander still had a few routines to play. As the manager or assistant came round the counter, or the emergency button was pressed, he could energetically pretend to join in the chase while obstructing as much as possible. Even down to being first outside immediately after Bimbo and pointing dramatically in the wrong direction: 'He went that way.'

And if, after all this, some hero – Geoff's term of abuse had almost lost its original ironic edge – still managed to give chase and make a capture, he'd be likely to find that there was almost immediately plain-clothes police assistance on hand. *Geoff.*

'Ah, thank you, Sir. Well done. I'll take over now. I'm a police officer.' And he'd really grab Bimbo's arm as they march off down the street, both holding their shoulders as stiffly as possible so no one could detect the quakes of laughter rippling through them.

There even was another cunning stroke to pull if the situation looked especially difficult – if the 'hero' and the crowd had a suspicious look about them. Geoff would go through his routine but would say. 'Now, Sir, would you mind holding on to this man for a moment while I phone for assistance. As tightly as you can.'

This would make room for a bit of wheedling and pleading

from Bimbo while Geoff was round the corner. 'Oh come on, give a fellow a chance. Before he gets back.'

Re-enter Sergeant Geoff. 'Thank you very much, Sir. You've been very helpful. You can leave the rest to me.'

Geoff himself had only had a short spell of prison in 20 years at this game. But that was not the most important matter to him. It was always the accomplice who took the greatest risks during the actual villainy and therefore it was *his* protection from tellers, managers and heroes which was paramount. It was upon this that Geoff's reputation finally rested. 'And nobody', he told me proudly, 'has ever got left behind.' And then, as though sensing that this was uncharacteristically histrionic, particularly as he'd had almost to shout it through the smoke and decibels of another Sunday at the Horse and Groom, he turned to John for a little professional support. 'Come on, John. You know don't you? In the end it's all a big fucking joke. Innit?'

Sometimes, when I've given seminars on 'The Criminal Subculture' and mentioned Geoff's little tricks, I've had one or two people in the audience questioning his capacity to deceive. 'Surely, no one would be fooled by that. Aren't they on the look-out for distractions in banks; wouldn't they suspect the sudden appearance of a plain-clothes policeman?' I try to answer by suggesting that perhaps there is something particularly unexpected about two apparent strangers being in league with each other. Sometimes, when the questioner looks as though he may have a theoretical bent, I even go on about the way in which the anonymity of contemporary urban life breeds this presumption of solitariness. But usually I rely on another con involving accomplices to help make the point – one which shook up my own clever ideas on the subject – the con surrounding the game of 'three-card monte' or 'find the lady'.

Like most other people, I've seen them working this little

dodge up and down Oxford Street during the tourist season. The dealer, usually standing behind a suitcase or a cardboard box, first of all holds up three cards for the crowd's inspection. One of these is a queen or other picture card. After a bit of chatter and chunter about this and that which helps to pass the time while the crowd builds up, he places the cards face downwards on the box and invite anyone to pick the queen, offering odds of 2–1 or even better to the successful person.

You don't need to be very smart to recognize that there's a confederate in the little crowd to help along the betting. Someone to encourage a hesitant tourist. 'Look it's easy. That card on the left. That's the queen. There. Told you so. Should have had some money on that.' In fact you can feel quite superior as you watch the game build up until the victim or victims, encouraged by the confederate, finally decides to have a go, and promptly loses all.

It took a week of nudging after our visit to the Horse and Groom, but John finally agreed to try and arrange for me to interview some of the people who were at this dodge. He knew the pub in Long Acre where the 'three-card' people drank.

But it was a difficult scene we encountered when we strolled in one Wednesday afternoon just half an hour before closing-time. Apart from John and myself, the rather drab little bar was empty except for a straggling group of about seven or eight men who were sprawled around tables and chairs over by the dartboard.

'Perhaps they're not here yet,' I consoled, after a mouthful of my pint.

'That's them,' he said.

'What, *all* of them?' I protested. 'There's at least eight.'

'That's them,' said John decisively, and sat still.

Although this situation was now becoming familiar, it never felt any more comfortable. The problem was that some of the people at the tables clearly knew John. Normally they'd have talked to him. But I was there. So they had to pretend not to know. Meanwhile, of course, John was gearing himself up to go across and speak to them in a manner he'd never used before. After the usual introductory, 'All right, Pete? How are things, George?' and a few laconic nods to the others, he'd somehow or other have to manage something like: 'Look, I've got this friend with me. Laurie Taylor. He's a professor, but he's all right. He wants to have a word with you about the game. Learn how it's done.'

That was what I guessed he was now uneasily rehearsing into the head of his Pils. I sat silent. I had the feeling that almost anything I said might be used as an excuse to abandon the project – there and then. It was nearly twenty minutes before he got up and made the short stroll down the bar. 'John! George! Pete!' Then quiet. A few people broke away from the group and leant uncomfortably on the bar as though they'd rather not watch Big John McVicar reading these sort of lines. Some shaking of heads in the group. John came back. I could tell from his face that he'd been through even more than he'd bargained for. 'You can watch if you keep your distance. But no talking at all. And definitely no interviews. Or recording. You've got to understand I know these people. This is their livelihood.' A minute later I saw piles of banknotes being distributed around the members of the group and then they were off to work. All together. A minute after that John muttered something about finding a copy of *Kind of Blue* in Dobell's and I was left to make my own way after the three-card repertory company.

For that's really what it was. A couple of men with those sort of shifty faces which come from having spent a lifetime looking through crowds for signs of danger. Like gazelles really. One moment savouring the delights of the three bottles of Chanel No. 4 which they are able to let you have at knock-down prices, and the next nervously sniffing the sidewalk for the scent of an approaching constable. (Of course, the apprehension is usually just part of salesmanship: something which helps the punters to believe that these must indeed be stolen goods. But it leaves its mark on the neck muscles.)

Alongside such predictable looking villains were a couple of people who could have passed as junior executives, a couple in greasy camel coats who looked like odd-job men, and even one passable impersonation of a tourist with shopping bag and camera in evidence.

I caught up with them just along from Centre Point outside a shop advertising American boots. The dealer, or the 'thrower' as he gets called, was already well into his chat, holding up three cards and showing them to the small crowd which had already gathered. I kept my distance by staring with more than usual interest at a display pair of Frye cowboy boots which seemed to boast a steel insert. It took me a moment to realize that this wasn't a small crowd at all. The dealer's audience consisted entirely of the gang, except for two members who seemed to have taken up positions as look-outs about 30 yards away on either side of the pitch. What was so alarming was that I'd often stood in crowds no bigger than this myself, when I'd been a 'student of the game' a few months before. There I'd been, in my little anonymous crowd, secure in the knowledge that unlike many of the mugs around me, I'd seen through the trickery and spotted the confederate. Whilst, in reality, I'd been virtually the only outsider in a tightly knit group of half a dozen villains who were all considering how to get into my wallet.

A few more genuine mugs had now joined the present group and I was able to drift onto the outside edge without feeling intrusive. Once again the cards were shown: a queen, a five of diamonds and a seven of spades. Although they were being moved around, it wasn't difficult to follow the queen and see exactly which one it was, when, after a few moments, the three cards were placed face down on the up-ended cardboard box. Then came the tricky bit: the dealer's hands slid the three cards backwards and forwards, rapidly changing their places to disguise the eventual position of the queen.

This game, like nearly all other ones I saw, then started with an accomplice or two placing bets, £5 or £10 notes on top of the chosen card in a fairly random way. Even though I wasn't always certain where the queen was after all the shuffling around, I felt – as I half-realized I was supposed to feel – that I could do better than they were doing. Mugs are indeed encouraged by just this fact, as well as by the generous odds which are being offered, and by the roll of money which the dealer adroitly holds in view while simultaneously displaying the cards. But if all that is not enough to get the mug's wallet out, then in come the one or two 'gees' whose job is literally to gee-up the victim. 'Look,' they say conspiratorially to him; 'You can spot the queen – it's got a little bend in the corner.' And yes, the dealer tips over the card with the bend; and queen it is. One of the gees bets heavily on the next game and wins.

The dealer looks a shade concerned. Now the mug is encouraged to stake. He may even be allowed to win while an accomplice's money placed on the wrong card is lost. The course of action depends on the amount in his wallet, which is communicated to the dealer so that the latter can time the final stroke. And then on to the only games which really count, when at last a chunk of the mug's own money is on the cards; sometimes almost pulled out of his wallet by an over-friendly gee desperately anxious that his new-found friend should share his apparent prosperity. 'Come on mate, stick it all on. Why not? Can't you see the bend in the corner?' And that's the game in which a bend mysteriously turns up on another card, while the queen with its own bend nicely concealed by the dealer's thumb, turns out to have moved elsewhere.

'Look out – the law!' says the dealer, and moves off left, with confederates scattering. One gee may even stay behind a second to cool things out. 'Hard luck, pal. I thought you had him there. Quick, before the police come. Don't want to get caught, do you?'

It was much the same outside HMV and Take Six as it was outside Saxone and Marks, but not until Selfridges and something like the tenth game did I stumble on the essence of the trick. Up till then I'd assumed that on the critical games the dealer just shuffled the cards around on the box rather more cleverly than before and used particularly distracting patter. But as we waited to find a clear space between the helium-balloon seller and the man with the jumping beans, I watched the dealer almost absent-mindedly shuffling the three cards. He was a young man compared to his accomplices. Aquiline. A bit like John Dankworth looked before he met Princess Margaret and stopped being Johnny. One – two – three. Down they went on top of the box. But face-up – unlike the actual game. Five of diamonds – seven of spades – queen. And again. But this time. Queen – five of diamonds – seven of spades. The Queen must have come from the bottom of the pack on that deal. Not a very novel little ploy, but only then did I at last realize that it was *here*, in the dealing of the cards onto the top of the box, and not in all the shuffling once they were there, that the trickery lay. All that shuffling was irrelevant, just there to allow a mug like me to feel he was fast enough to spot the movement of a card. But such skill was of no use if the card he was so carefully following was not in fact the queen.

Some mugs, of course, suspected trickery, knew that they'd successfully kept their eye on the queen during the shuffling. One Indian youth became particularly incensed and tried to break through to inspect the cards. This was the signal for some instant 'crowd control'. All the accomplices present showed great indignation at the youth's persistence:

'bad sport,' they called out with unlikely spontaneity. 'Be a good loser.' But it was often enough to get others in the crowd to join in.

At least these hypocrites had their moments of sentimentality. Outside the Academy cinema, I saw one accomplice actually preventing an elderly Cypriot lady from putting the contents of her purse on the card. 'No, no. Save your money, lady,' he said, pushing the notes back into her purse and almost physically propelling her towards the doors of M and S. 'Go and buy something with it.'

Near the end of the afternoon one little variation on the usual routine was thrown in almost as though to relieve the boredom. The dealer allowed himself to be distracted by an altercation to the left, perhaps, I couldn't quite see, by one of the shifty look-outs. A confederate promptly stepped forward and bent the corner of the queen without the dealer 'noticing'. He then positively tiptoed back into the crowd with a finger to his lips and a big melodramatic wink at the mug he'd been standing by previously.

I couldn't keep any sort of check on the illicit gains. So much 'stage' money – usually fives and tens – was passing backwards and forwards between accomplices and dealer that it was difficult to spot the real stuff. But when I spoke to John on the phone that evening, I said I thought it would be about a grand. 'Not bad for three hour's work,' I chattered.

'The dealer takes half,' he said. 'And most of that'll go away again this evening in the same space of time at the dogs.'

He sounded tetchy. Did he rather disapprove of the three-card monte gang just because this was the one occasion where I'd successfully played boy detective – fearless sociologist – and tracked down some material for myself?

'Well, it's still good money,' I insisted.

'Too much like hard work.'

'Yes. But it's clever, John. People think there's another card, or that it's done in the shuffling. But it's not.'

'No?'

'Oh no. If you watch carefully, you can see the way the queen goes down on the deck last rather than first.'

'Really?'

'Oh yes. Actually, the opposite of dealing off the bottom of the pack when you think about it.'

'Mmm.'

I was determined to press home my advantage. I even suspected that he hadn't known how the trick was done. He certainly hadn't said anything about it before. 'It's nothing but sleight of hand.'

'In that case,' said John, sounding decisive for the first time, 'it won't be of much use to you as a criminologist. That just about makes it legal.'

I began to suspect that my new knowledge of the special potency of accomplices had been gained at some expense. In the field of criminological research, life was becoming increasingly solitary.

4

ENTER ROBBERS ARMED

In which John plays old times – the author learns why grasses don't get cut – why shotguns are safer than coshes – and how ex-bank robbers deal with boredom.

I was beginning to wish Phil would find something else to look at. It was nearly ten minutes since John McVicar had introduced me and explained my interest in talking to him about his career as an armed robber. But there he was, a big broad-shouldered man, still staring at me as he talked, as though I was a recalcitrant bank manager. I decided it might be some sort of credibility test – hadn't I read somewhere in the American subcultural literature about 'facing out'? – and tried to smile back like a man of the world. It was not easy, particularly as he now seemed to have picked up on John's introduction – 'This is Laurie Taylor. He's a professor.' – and to be holding me personally responsible for sociology.

'I did sociology in the nick,' he said aggressively. I toyed with a response which referred to such other successful graduates as John McVicar, Charlie Richardson and Wally Probyn, but decided to stick to silence and an urbane smile.

'Yeah. I used it as a way of conditioning myself.'

My face said 'interesting'.

'Punishment in the gym on the weights. And punishment in the cell reading your books.'

I managed an approving nod. What the hell were my books to me anyway?

The attack switched unexpectedly. 'I used to read Chinoy from front to back. [Ely Chinoy is the author of *Society: an introduction to sociology*.] I'm probably the only person in the world to ever do that.'

I vaguely felt that something defensive was called for, although I'd never come across Chinoy, and could remember nothing whatsoever about his fat introductory text except that there was a picture of Lena Horne somewhere near the front with a caption about 'racial integration in the world of entertainment'. I waited for the next punch. It came.

'You know what I've always wanted to do to a criminologist. I'd like to get a criminologist. Say to him. "Right. You think you're a fucking expert on crime. I want to show you what it's really like." Not something big. Not a bank. Just stealing a car. Go out and steal a car with him, make him steal a car, so he'd know how it feels – what it feels like – then perhaps he'd understand: wouldn't have to have so many fucking theories.'

I wondered if Phil's confrontational style was having a particularly strong effect on me because of the weeks I'd spent with con men, with people whose professional work involved drawing attention away from themselves. Geoff and Les may have liked to get their laughs down at the Horse and Groom or the Landsdowne, but they certainly had no wish to make any lasting personal impression on anyone when they went to work. The highest compliment to their professional skills was to have a bank teller not only fail to remember anything about their appearance, but also forget any details whatsoever of the brief exchange which had cost the bank several hundred pounds.

When Phil made his dramatic entrance, the effect was rather different. He didn't slide quietly into a bank, and spend five or ten minutes surreptitiously 'clocking' the tellers and trying to gauge their degree of gullibility. Together with a trio of heavies, he kicked his way straight to the counter with a fury which was precisely calculated to secure prompt and total submission. This was 'fronting up': as much a piece of practised and evaluated technique for the armed robber as distraction was for the con man.

I wasn't too sorry to find Phil relatively difficult company. After a few weeks of talking to con men, I could feel my morality being overpowered by their anarchic repertory of tricks and fiddles, their scandalous disrespect for bank managers, solicitors and business executives, their shameless delight in exploiting the cupidity of normally law-abiding citizens. Armed robbery promised to leave me much greater space for ethical disapproval.

John, as far as I could tell, was enjoying it more than usual. He'd worked with Phil during his last period as a robber, so he must have known exactly the sort of reception that a sociologist with a cassette-recorder was likely to receive. After my evident delight at the jolly subversiveness of the con men, he was probably rather happy watching my liberal sensibilities trying to grapple with this type of crass villainy.

'It's OK, innit?' Phil had mistaken my temporarily averted eyes for an interest in his flat. Well yes, it was OK. But really I was wondering if I'd ever seen quite such an extravagant display of bad taste. A fitted carpet with bright lime-green whirls on an emerald-green background seemed more suited to an ice-cream parlour than a living-room, while everywhere else you looked the eye was caught by enormous cut-glass and china ornaments: swans, peacocks, bowls of coloured fruit, cornucopias. All this, together with the numerous plaster-of-paris statues which were dotted in gnomic formations between chairs and tables, suggested a good day's winnings on an up-market coconut shy. I wondered, however, if my sudden rush of aesthetic sensibility was really a way of getting a little edge on the dangerous Phil.

'Worth 90 grand. Got another place in Sussex. Elizabethan manor house.' I wasn't given a second to imagine the likely depredations: they were piled up for my approval. 'Oh yes. At this moment I'm in the middle of gutting the interior: ripping out all the old stuff so as to have room for a full-size snooker table.' It was all quite true, John explained later –

right down to the flying ducks which Phil had lovingly pointed out to him in one of the oak-panelled rooms. Neither was it an elaborate exercise in kitsch. Phil's whole way of being in the world was 'fronting up': bank tellers, visiting sociologists, preservationists – they were all fair game.

But at least, now that he'd taken my measure – used his clear blue eyes to get me sitting up like a frightened rabbit – he started straight into answers without waiting for my first question. I suppose it was his way of sorting out interviewers.

'You're a criminologist, Laurie.'

I nodded uneasily.

'I'll tell you something you don't know. There's only 50 people in this country with the ability, facilities and temperament to go out and rob a bank. People who've had the training. Well, there's a lot more, but they're all inside. But I'd say the hard core for that type of crime is 50. You, John, would know 30 of those people and I'd know 20. The rest would be known to each other.'

John was looking a little uncertain. This was his area as well as Phil's.

'Oh no, John – it *is* complicated. Fucking complicated. Oh yeah. Certainly to an everyday person.' He didn't have to look far to find a handy example. 'Take Laurie. If I said to Laurie. 'OK, let's rob a bank.' Even if he has the ability and even the facilities, what he hasn't got is the training, the expertise.'

John still shook his head unhappily. I wondered why he'd chosen to take issue with his ex-partner over the matter. Surely he'd be only too happy to allow that some special skills had been needed in his long criminal career? Nobody was more likely than him to look down upon the petty thieves he referred to as gas-meter bandits or the undisciplined robbers who were dismissed as cowboys.

'Come on, John. People don't ... you know, you don't get people at 35 years of age getting together and saying, 'Right, we'll rob a bank. Which one shall we do? Right off we go.' On television they do. But it doesn't happen.'

When John disagrees, he gets quieter. Eventually he just sits there silently until the person he disagrees with modifies or qualifies his position. It was refreshing to see someone else being wound up by it for a change. Phil tried the shot from another angle.

'Look, John. You know and I know what it's like when you get under pressure – for those three minutes – when the coup is on, when you've got the whole weight of the Metropolitan police and the whole of the world's resources against you. When it's just four of you against the world for those three minutes. A lot of them just fall to bits.'

John nodded. We were back in conversational business. And I realized his objection to Phil's 'training'. It got in the way of the characteristic that he wanted right at the centre of the enterprise. All right, you might have to learn a few simple things to go to work as a robber, but these could be picked up by anyone in a couple of hours; they were as nothing alongside that essential characteristic of 'nerve'. That was what kept the number of armed robbers down to 50. That was what he'd shared with Phil.

'You mean the robbers have got to have *macho*?' (I pronounced it 'matcho' the way they did at the Landsdowne Club.) Up went Phil's eyebrows.

'Not at all.' He pulled himself up from the plump depths of his armchair. 'He's got to be the right guy under pressure. That's all. I used to go to work with a little poofy homosexual weakling who was absolutely superb. I've seen others – big men – who couldn't do it. Their nerve went.'

He reminded John of a bank robbery in Islington. (Unlike con men, robbers don't always go in for 'Lloyds' or 'Barclays': their raids are sufficiently few and far between to

be remembered by place. 'Were you on the Wembley job?'
'Oh yes, wasn't he the one that did Hammersmith.') On the
Islington raid, this 'little poofy weakling' – Michael – was
squeezed into a children's pram, pushed into the bank by one
of the gang and then left to leap out at the critical moment to
add his share of terror.

But wasn't that macho in a way, I wanted to know? Being
tough. Ready for action.

'No, no, no!' John and Phil were back together again.
'Robbers are into risks,' John explained. 'That's their game.
They're not into combat for its own sake. That sort of macho
is what you find in a gangster. *Risk* and *combat*.' He
underlined the terms for me. And started to write the
paragraphs. 'That's the distinction between robbers and
gangsters, between people like Phil here and Ronnie Kray.'

I persisted. 'I'm sure most people would call it macho
though. All that crashing into the bank and firing guns.'

'Yeah, but that's only the couple of minutes you're in the
bank,' insisted Phil.

'Well, then, there's all the rushing out, jumping into
getaway cars and screaming off through red lights.' I knew
my Sweeney, all right.

Phil went measured. Almost pedantic. 'No, no. In many
many circumstances you never drive fast away from
anywhere. That's almost a rule.'

'But surely you choose people because they're crack
drivers?'

'No. You choose drivers because they're people who will
sit there nice and cool outside the bank while all those
fireworks are happening in there and the police are coming
down the road. The most important thing in a driver is that
he stays there and never leaves you. Remember Luton, John?'

'What was that?' I could see John half wanted to play old
times with Phil, particularly when it would help to make a
point against me, but he hesitated.

'That one that looked impregnable,' said Phil. John still hesitated.

'Why was it impregnable?' I asked Phil.

'Because . . . because . . . well because it was a big clearing bank for the area, so you not only had tellers and all that, you had people up on the balcony walking around.'

John capitulated. Enthusiastically. '*Yeah*. What about when I pulled that shot-gun out. Just before I pulled it out, I was on the way in. I'm in the doorway. And this geezer was . . .'

'Oh yes. He was coming out.'

'That's right, Phil. He was the gasman, wasn't he? He had a bagful of shillings that he'd been changing. I said, "Oh excuse me a moment." In the doorway. He went: "Oh yes, certainly." And he backed off and I pulled the shot-gun out.'

'But you let him out of the bank. He went off.'

'Did I?' John was laughing now. 'Did I let him out?'

'Yeah. I had to go out and run down the road and bring him back in again. And then I took his money off him.'

'Did you?' John rubbed his hands together at the memory. 'You took that little bag of shillings? All his gas money?'

It was the first of several similar 'jokes' that I was to hear from bank robbers. If somebody could stage-manage a bit of unnecessary business while the raid was on, such as the theft of a useless bag of shillings, then it assured everyone else in the gang that the situation was well under control. It was a sign of quiet confidence, of relaxation at the moment of greatest tension.

'And we got away from that one *very very slow*, didn't we John? It was a very successful bank robbery. No big tearaway. We were in and out and presented people with a *fait accompli* and nobody was hurt. Really, Laurie. If you look at the court transcript of that case, you'll see it was a classically successful robbery.' He showed no recognition of how his words undermined his claim.

I was still wary of Phil. The 'jokes' didn't seem all that funny, and much of his talk seemed to carry a challenge: go on, say it wasn't successful; go on, prove I'm not as brave or clever as I'm telling you I am. I must have been feeling a little sorry for some of the people he'd worked with, for I heard myself muttering: 'But what about those who haven't got the nerve, who can't stand the pace? How can you find them out before you go on a job?'

'You have to force them to work,' said Phil. 'I remember this one you weren't on, John. Richmond. I knew they weren't keen. But they wouldn't say a word. *Daren't*. I was with them all in this motorway café on the morning. Me eating a big breakfast, double egg, bacon, tomato, sopping up the grease on the plate with bread – while they nibbled their toast. I knew they'd get on the plot [the scene of the action] and find all sorts of clues to swallow it. "Oh, look at this and that." But they'd do it in such a way that nobody could accuse them of bottling out when we got back. I knew this. *I knew it*. And I thought, right, I'm going to force you bastards into that bank when we arrive.

'And when we got on the plot, and they were working up some excuses to pull off, I just went in. I went in, and they had to follow me. They *had* to come in. They had to come – otherwise their lives would've been destroyed.'

'Why?' I asked.

'The *stigma* of course. *Rats* . . . They're no longer bank robbers if they didn't come in that bank. *And they came in.* Even if it was a full 30 seconds late, with me – can you imagine it? – stuck there in the middle of the bank, by myself. Every second seemed like an hour. *But I shamed them into it.*' And then, with withering contempt: 'I shamed them – those super-duper bank robbers with their arse-holes gone.'

On the face of it, an extravagantly decorated lounge on the third floor of a luxury block of flats in Knightsbridge should have been a relatively relaxing place to talk about such alarming matters as professional robbery. And indeed it was for short periods of time. But quite suddenly Phil would become unduly exercised about some small matter: who it was who jumped over the counter in Guildford; how much the share-out was after the Purley job; who was slow getting out of the car in Lewisham. And then he'd bang the table in front of him in such a vigorous manner that it set up a terrible death-rattle among the elaborate glass ornaments which adorned it. It may have been another instance of what John called my liberal sensitivity, but it did seem to me that any man who treated his property with such little caution would have scant respect for items which others might hold dear to them – like, say, arms and legs.

When Phil wasn't banging the table, or staring me out, or trying to get John to play old times, he liked to talk about adrenalin. In fact, as far as I could gather he held a quantum theory of the stuff, according to which there was only a certain amount available in the world, and most of this had been cornered by professional criminals, and in particular the armed robber. Adrenalin was something that got you going: you could feel the adrenalin rising, and once the adrenalin started, then all the anxieties and concerns of the everyday world began to move aside.

'Remember that feeling, John? When the adrenalin starts. On the morning itself. Right? When you start laying it all out.'

I knew from experience that all this was a shade too romantic for John, but faced with a choice between my evident pusillanimity and his ex-partner's rising adrenalin, there was only one way to go. He nodded appreciatively.

Phil addressed himself to the table. 'Right. Two sets of gloves. There. Clean all your silver coins in case you need them for the telephone. Clean your watch in case the glass gets broke.'

'Labels,' reminded John.

'*Labels off all clothes*. Lay it all out. Everything spotless. All the guns cleaned. All the cartridges cleaned. Everything absolutely clean. Cos you're vulnerable from that time on.'

I didn't say anything at that moment because it might have been misconstrued, but I could remember reading another armed robber's account of the clear-headed feeling which the rising adrenalin was supposed to bring as the time for action got nearer:

> Any nervous tension I used to feel before a job didn't stay with me all the time. Only till I got started. Once I start I feel completely calm, one hundred per cent, everything comes brilliant to me ... I might be fogged up a minute or two before, but the minute it's on, it's like the sun coming out from behind a cloud.

Certainly the sun no longer shone in the criminal world for the author of that little piece, supergrass Bertie Smalls. John had, nevertheless, liked the description when I read it to him, though he backed away a little from its overromanticism. This was the difficulty that he was in at that moment with Phil's interview. Of course, he knew there was something mythical about the usual picture of the big-time robber. He'd spent years trying to distance himself from the press description of his dangerousness. Despite heavy pressure from editors and television producers he still tried hard not to trade upon the image which could so often get in the way of any proper appreciation of his present journalistic work.

But this didn't mean that he was happy to go along with any 'labelling' version of his life that I might be peddling – an account in which most of the drama of the robbery was to be found in the constructions which had been placed upon it by film and television over the years. There was a reality about his nerve, his toughness, his staunchness, which had to be protected. And there were ways in which he enjoyed the reputation which preceded him.

His early release from prison, he believed, owed more to the Home Office's fear of the trouble he could cause, than in any belief in his reformation. And in pubs and clubs he was pleased to allow his name to count. I recall one rainy night standing in a queue outside the Comedy Store in Soho. A mob of people were, as usual, trying to force their way through the narrow doorway and into the tiny lift which would eventually take them up to their seats. But someone inside had been checking the reservations list and out came the commissionaire – 'John McVicar's party, please.' The sea parted. John put his head up and strolled casually forward, while the rest of us followed blindly in his wake. I knew from his face on this occasion that it was not his wish to be given such treatment but he was hard pushed to ignore the impact that his name still made.

Phil sensed a bit of this ambiguity about John's present life. Even though he himself now lives luxuriously on the proceeds of legitimate business (albeit one initially financed by loot from bank raids), he still talks about crime as an immediate option, something which he is likely to go back to at any moment, and he seemed to enjoy telling stories which might bring John back into the fold, arouse his latent sympathies even if I was the immediate object of them.

'Picture this, Laurie. True story. We've robbed a bank. Richmond. Come away. We've had a chase-up by the police. Lost 'em. Now we're in the car. Locked up though in this garage on a council estate just up the road. We think we're sweet until we hear the police radios outside. They know we're in one of the twenty lock-ups. I know I'm on fifteen years if I get caught.'

'Had to be so quiet while they prowled round. That's how I went bald, I think, knowing that I was in this poxy garage with them all out there breaking open garage doors to get at us. We kept very quiet. I'm in the car. Engine on. And the second they opened our door, I came out in reverse. Pushed the police cars aside. They were like Dinky toys. Firing shots and throwing truncheons!'

John nodded. The message from his face was: 'You don't get me back as easy as that, Phil. I know you got caught for that job. Went to prison.'

Phil seemed to read it as clearly as I did because he went for the one aspect of the story which kept the status of the armed robber in capital letters.

'I'll tell you something, Laurie. In the police colleges, it's OK to nick a motorist; but the prize, the mythological prize, is the bank robber. For a policeman to catch a bank robber is like a fisherman catching a 20 lb trout. When they got me, they was bringing people in to look. "Look, we've got this bank robber. *Look at him*." You know.' Phil broke into song as John nodded his head and began to laugh. 'The king is in his altogether ... his altogether ... They were walking round me: "Look, he's only flesh and blood."'

It was also clear to Phil that if armed robbers didn't arouse this sort of fear and animosity among others, then it was their role to go around creating it. He'd been astounded by the positive lack of attention he got in one prison.

'Honest, John, I just couldn't believe how these prisoners treated me. I really couldn't. I went to a place where they never have bank robbers. I was walking around and no one was curtseying. I mean, if I'm in Durham or Wandsworth, there are accepted strata. Bank robbers at the top. The prison authorities like it because it makes for easier running. But here, I was totally disorientated, because they didn't accept the kudos which was attached to being a bank robber, and, you know, serving a decade in prison. All these guys had been in months as opposed to years. I'll tell you, John. I had to act up and create again. You know. "Fuck off, you screws!" Start bashing a couple. Show my disregard for prison.'

There was malt whisky on the table. It had been circulating freely for the last half hour in glass tumblers which were so heavy that I could feel the strain in the muscles of my forearm as I gingerly lowered mine to the surface of the glass table.

Phil now poured another round, but kept his head down while he did so to indicate that he wanted a little dramatic silence before his next revelation. The bottle banged down on the table and he looked up. By now, John was looking distinctly unsociological.

'I get pissed off, John. Don't you? I've got the Rolls Royce, this flat, house in the country. I've bought a croquet set . . . so you can come down to croquet. But I'm bored. Really bored. Look, Laurie. Switch off that thing, will you. You'll have to remember this. And no names.'

He'd been so bored, he explained, that only a few weeks before we talked he'd got involved in an elaborate con which had gone seriously wrong. He'd had no need to take part. He'd just made it obvious down at one of the clubs that he was ready for some action and it had been put his way. It was all too close for him to want to give out any details, but from what I could gather it was a 'sting': an elaborately contrived con in which the victim, an Iraqi business man, had been offered some particularly valuable diamonds at below the market price. Phil's job had been to use his perfectly genuine social and financial aplomb to give the victim the right degree of confidence in the transaction. It was only after all his elaborate work – the trips to Le Gavroche and the Connaught to allow Phil to be greeted by head-waiters, the visits to banks where Phil was equally well-known – that the switch would be worked. The victim would hand his money over to an agreed third party (on the face of it a solicitor nominated by Phil, but in fact another member of the gang sitting in a hired office with dud name-plate) and in return would receive the suitcase of diamonds, which upon eventual inspection would turn out to be not those which had originally been offered for sale, but worthless replicas.

The irony of it all wasn't lost on Phil. There he was in a hotel suite in Kensington, pretending to be a plutocratic business man, when that was just what he was, risking ten years imprisonment by attempting to swindle some greedy mug for a personal gain which amounted to rather less than he could earn legitimately in a month. That was if all went well. But it didn't.

'He tumbled just as we were making the exchange. I saw his chauffeur slipping out of the room to get to the phone. And I'm sitting there. And I'm thinking. *What on earth am I doing here again*? Right in the fucking middle of it. Ten years. I just sat there almost wanting to say to this mug, "Look, I'm going to be a millionaire in two years' time. I don't want the money." But I came out of it and ran. I had to really run. And I'm right in the heart of embassy land. And all of a sudden I'm running down a cul-de-sac. And I can't go back. What am I doing? What *am* I doing?

'There was nothing for it. I had to dive through someone's window. Go through a house to get out the other side. And the people were in there watching television when "crash", I come straight through and out the back and home.'

'But, John.' He got all the encouragement he needed from John's face. 'It was just magic to be back.'

It's not only armed robbers who tell you that being 'at the heavy' is something special. I noticed in clubs and spielers that all other professional criminals deferred to the successful robber. A great deal of this status obviously derived from the independence and spontaneity of the activity. Although information was often vital, and someone had to help you to 'tool up' with guns and other weapons before the big day, once you decided to go you were completely on your own. Out in the open. Exposed. You couldn't back away like a con man, or a hoister or a burglar, and pretend that really you hadn't intended to run across the pavement waving a sawn-off shot-gun at a security guard.

It was also fast. In a matter of minutes, you could earn more money than a hoister or burglar might knock up in six months illegal hustling. But perhaps most important as far as other villains were concerned – it was a high-risk game.

In this culture, everyone gambles. Horses, dogs, boxing, kalooki, poker, brag. You always try to know the odds. In armed robbery they aren't good. Not only do you risk a ten to fifteen-year sentence (longer than any other professional crime), but your chances of being caught are high, so high in fact that I could not find a single example of a robber who had not at some time in his career served a sentence of at least eight years.

These were the reasons, rather than anything about the intrinsic activity itself – firing guns, driving fast cars – which made robbery an acknowledged breeding-ground for those values which other professional criminals liked to cite as their own. Ideas about how a robber would behave in a dangerous situation, – how he would face up to trouble, spend his money, share out his loot, serve his 'time', dispatch his enemies, treat his women, look after his friends – were guides for every career-criminal, from the pickpocket on the Central Line to gentlemen fraudsters hard at work in the bowels of the city. And within this ideal set of values, nothing ranked higher than 'loyalty' or lower than 'grassing'.

The condemnation is absolute: informing is the treason of the criminal world. Indeed, to the extent that a criminal has a distinctive identity, that identity is founded on a definition of the self which excludes not only informing, but even the capability of being an informer. You have to know that you couldn't do it. But something had gone wrong in recent years with this central value.

It wasn't a subject I needed to raise in this company. No

sooner did Phil or John seek to extol the strengths or virtues of their one-time way of life, than they ran up against the appalling fact that several of their most notorious colleagues at the game had 'cracked'. 'Supergrasses' had in the last ten years systematically informed on so many members of their former gangs that many villains had almost come to share the police's view of the precariousness of the enterprise. How could they have done it? Phil spoke of his last arrest.

'They were fucking savage with me. Had me handcuffed to a chair. Sticking their guns in me and battering me. Plastic bucket over the head, smashing it with their truncheons', adding for my benefit, 'it doesn't mark the face.'

'They wanted information. Pushing my head down the toilet where one of them had had a shit. The doctor was quite shocked when he looked at what they'd done. They had to take him away and show him the guns and money to justify their behaviour.'

'Did you get near to cracking,' asked John, as bound up in this issue as in anything we'd ever discussed in these interviews.

'No. Something about it being all physical. When it's just physical, you can become . . . it's a funny thing this . . . you can use the physical thing the other way round . . . to increase your own resolution.'

'Yes, that's it,' said John. 'I made my stand on not answering the very first question. They said. "What's your name?" They knew it, but it was their way of starting. *And mine*. They sticked and punched and kicked me, but a lot of the time they were just getting in each other's way. I never fought back. They wanted some justification for what they were doing. They had to have something to keep them going. One of them kept chuntering on about the charge I'd been arrested on: "You bastard cunt. Shooting at an unarmed bobby." I knew they had to have him saying that to keep them going. And knowing it helped me to hang on. Then you got to the stage where they're hitting you on the injuries you've already got.'

Phil nodded sympathetically.

'So I played the head game of taking it one blow at a time. I hung on to the thought that they'd got to stop some time, so if *I could keep quiet for one more blow, then it would stop*.'

In their different ways John and Phil were happy to disown many of their fellow villains. John spent less and less time with them; had grown tired of their cultural insularity. Phil even spoke of being 'contemptuous of them'. But both had no doubt at all that their lives would have been ruined if they'd grassed. This loyalty wasn't just a bit of dispensable ideology; it was at the heart of their present identities. It was a loyalty which they both saw as especially true of the criminal world, even though both had been witness to what Phil called 'enough treachery to fill twenty volumes of Shakespeare'.

I didn't want to gloat, but I so rarely enjoyed any sense of advantage in these encounters that I couldn't resist pressing my question about why so many people grassed, especially if, as they kept saying, this loyalty was so marked among those who were at the heavy.

Phil wriggled a bit on the hook and tried to find some qualification which might keep the full impact of such betrayal at bay. There was one famous supergrass, for example, who could have fingered *him*.

'But, he didn't grass his real mates. He never would have. I mean, I never would have dreamt he'd do it. And he did everybody. But a few people he left out. His real mates.'

It went quiet while we all contemplated the inadequacy of Phil's excuse. To break the silence I asked if there was anything in common among those people who have grassed. The mood was so lugubrious by this time that, quite unusually, my question was just taken aboard by John and Phil as though I was a fellow conversationalist rather than an outsider.

John mused. 'Some of them are very strong people. Look at Bert [Bertie Smalls]. He was a good worker, although there was always something odd about him. He'd . . . he used to like to go out with girls who were 'on'. He liked rubbing the blood all over him. He was always a bit funny and he'd been a ponce as well. Then there's Andy . . . he's fucking queer.'

This sounded too much like special pleading to me. Was it really only sexual deviants who were likely to grass? What about new police techniques? Mightn't these now have been improved to the point where anyone could be broken?

'It's a case of getting you at the right time with the right thing,' said Phil quietly. 'Like Koestler's *Spanish Testament*. Have you read it? I always think I might have cracked if they'd got everything right.'

Although it hardly seemed much of an admission, it was deep into frightening territory as far as John was concerned. He wanted reassurance from his ex-partner.

'But how would you have felt if you'd cracked?'

'Oh destroyed. *Destroyed*. You know. I'm so pleased that I didn't.'

In this context, there was something almost touchingly unheroic about Phil's statement; enough, perhaps, to nudge John into his own story.

'They came at me once,' he recalled. 'It was so clever and devious that even now I have to admire it. I mean I'd been nicked bang to rights. I'd just come off a robbery and some members of the Yard swooped on me for something else and caught me with everything in my hand but a signed confession. They caught me with money from the raid, a cosh with incriminating hair and blood on it, clothing that matched a description of one of the robbers, and a mask. Two of the Yard had me in a corner of the charge-room in the police station while 20 uniformed coppers looked on. I went straight into the most approachable looking of the two

detectives. Quietly. "Look. Can I talk business with you?"
Back he came. A whisper. "No. The only thing you can talk
is a statement. You're gone. You've no chance, and you get
no help." I really panicked. "Look, I can put a chunk in your
hand within a couple of hours. A big chunk." He choked me
off. "Give us some bodies and we might get you a couple of
years off the fifteen we're lining up for you." Then they
stripped off my clothes, handcuffed my hands behind my
back, and slung me in a cell. They just left me there for hours.
Stewing in my own demoralized juice.'

I had the feeling, and judging by his silence so did Phil, that
this wasn't a reflection to interrupt. It was the story of how
near John had come to breaking, and was being told for his
benefit – not ours.

'When they came again, I was at a low ebb. "John. We
don't have to tell you what we've come up with. Money, the
car, overalls, the cosh ... you've got no chance." They
pulled the door to and were standing in the middle of the cell
looking at me. The detective who was talking seemed
suddenly to be very reasonable and I felt the germ of a money
deal in the air. "Well," I said, "I know the strength, but can't
we do something?"

'"First of all, you must know that you just can't walk out
of this one. You've gotta go away. The thing is, for how
long. It could be a fifteen and if you get a kind judge, maybe
ten. But with some help it could be a five, or even a four." He
shrugged, opened his hands like a market trader making a
final offer, then went on. "What we could do is drop the
attempted murder, sweeten up the robbery charge – make
you the driver or something. And whatever mitigation you
can put together, we'll support. A four is a lot different than a
fourteen." He just let the thought hang in the air.

'I began to smell a rat. What exactly were we talking about?
All these pauses were a bit contrived, the sentences a bit
practised, if we were talking about the usual sort of deal.

"What do you want?" I went on. "What kind of money do you want?"

'And then I saw how gently they'd led me to the point: "John, you're respected, really respected, and you know everyone. The deal we're offering you is to give us information. Just me and my mate here. That's all. No one else will ever know what's going on." I didn't hesitate. I rushed in. But I think that really I was so quick because I had to stifle a dreadful temptation. "Look. You're insulting me." "Look, John," he goes, as though he was reading a script and he knew his exact cues. "Don't give us your answer now. Think about it. We're not asking you to go into the box or to put your close mates in it. We just want a little information to help us get on in our jobs. And if you help us, we'll help you." Then he threw his last sprat. On cue again. "You don't think you'd be the only one, do you? You'd be amazed if you knew." He turned to leave. Then at the door: "We'll come back later." And I was shaking when they'd gone because I could see how clever it had been. Very clever.'

I didn't want to press any further on grassing. I'd seen Phil and John both contemplate the possibility and draw back in horror at what it would have done to their lives – although both of them might have spent a decade less in prison if they'd managed even a little secret co-operation. And I remembered the police sergeant's description of Bertie Smalls, after he'd made the statement at Wembley that was to send about 20 of his former friends off to prison for a total of 300 years: 'Like a caged animal. Walking up and down. Never still. And sweat poured off him. In fact during the last 48 hours of the statement taking, he had not even had a shave. His eyes were red. He was shaking and he was continuously wiping his forehead and face with a handkerchief.'

I didn't find all this police attention to armed robbers half as problematic as John or Phil. It was surely a question of violence. That cosh with hair and blood on it. Surely no other type of professional criminal – not even the average gangster – went out and physically assaulted the people who were simply doing their job, or who happened to be in the way when the heavy mob stormed in. Wasn't the police reaction natural? Weren't they little more than bullies? That certainly got Phil's eyes back on me.

'Oh, no! Good God! No! I used to say if a guy's carrying a lot of money, then I'll fight him. But that's it. Yes, there's other types of criminals who're thugs and bullies and push people about. But as long as people recognize who you are, as long as they say, "Here's a bank robber who knows his business," then there's no trouble. I like to think of myself as a cultured criminal as opposed to the caricature of the drinking, fighting, fucking person.'

'But surely', I persisted, "you only get people to recognize who you are by threatening them – by bullying them – waving a gun in their faces. The fact that you don't actually use it doesn't make much difference.'

'Hell, yeah.' Phil seemed on the edge of some concession. 'Remember that Securiguard, John? You know, the guy with the money chained on the wrist and you go, "Shall I shoot the chain off?" and the guy says "No, no, no, *please*. Look, undo the . . . the . . . it unclips." Cos I was holding it and you were going to shoot it. Remember?'

Questions of fine morality receded in the pleasure of recollection. John gave him the nod he wanted and on he went.

'And the guy goes, "No, no *please*. It unclips. Look. There you are.' His fist came down on the table and the ornaments shivered apprehensively. It was too close to the bone for John to participate – at least in my presence. Phil climbed back into the interview framework and out of the ebullience of yesterday's coups.

'Yes, well, thinking back. Retrospectively. It was . . . erm . . . erm . . . you know, barbaric to say the least. What we did.'

'You really believe that?' John pressed gently. Phil had relaxed completely again.

'Yeah, I do. I think it was fucking diabolical.'

For a second I thought I'd misjudged him. Here he was drawing back from just the type of macho bullying which even John clung to as part of his thoroughgoing masculinity.

'*Fucking diabolical*,' said Phil again, but this time he accompanied it with a roar of laughter and his fist smashed the table an inch from the glass swan.

For some time after talking to Phil, I had this recurrent image of myself sitting in a car outside a bank muttering something about not feeling quite up to it at the moment and would anyone mind if I sat this one out, while the ferocious Phil stood inside the bank firing shots into the ceiling and waiting for me to show.

For, despite all Phil's talk about poofy homosexual weaklings being able to take part in this sort of game, I had developed a fairly tight view of the sort of characters who gravitated towards it. Both John and Phil had this necessity to take on the world, to dare it to do its worst to them. Armed robbery provided them with a concentrated opportunity – a lightning sketch – in which this conflict could be dramatized: those few moments, when, to use Phil's phrase, 'you knew the whole world was against you' but there you stood out in the street or in the middle of the bank, defying all comers. I might have settled for this interpretation – believed it true for all robbers – if John hadn't seen the way things were going and taken me over to meet Derek.

Although John described him as just as successful a robber as Phil or himself, and having had just as many years at the game, he had no luxury flat and certainly no expensive ornaments to show for it. Quite the opposite. He lived in a small council flat in Stoke Newington. On the third floor of a five-storey block.

We arrived at Sunday lunchtime and sat down with Derek and his wife, Maureen, to a Sunday lunch of roast beef and Yorkshire pudding washed down with a flagon of Mateus Rosé. There was some inconsequential chat about who was doing this and that, a little fuss over who should have the last potato, a brief debate about the merits of a rat-faced mongrel dog which made an enthusiastic entry while we were on the apple crumble, and then Derek simply said, 'Well, shall we go and do this thing, John.' He led the way into a tiny room with just enough space for two single divans. John and I sat side by side on one, and Derek faced us on the other.

For three hours Derek talked in a rather sad, flat way about life as a bank robber. Much of what he had to say paralleled Phil's in content; but it was always less dramatic. Like Phil, he'd encountered reluctant bank robbers, had had his freedom imperilled by them, but he seemed to lack any sense of outrage.

'Yeah. I went to work with someone once. He never got out of the car. Couldn't get out of the car. Blind panic. I mean, if you try to open a car door handle this way and it won't open, you try to open it the other way don't you? And I was saying, "Well, leave that door and get out of the other door." You know. But by the time we'd been in and done it and come back and got in the motor again, he was still sitting there saying "I can't get this door open. I can't get this door open." And when we got to where we changing over [cars] someone still had to push it down for him. It was weird. As though he'd just gone.'

'Like frozen,' said John. 'People freeze, don't they? They don't exactly freeze through nerves. Sometimes it's as though they freeze through overstimulation. I've seen that, it's almost as though too much is hitting them. They get sluggish. Shell-shocked.' Derek chose to ignore this dramatic interpretation and stuck to the details.

'Yeah, this one just sat there trying the door one way.'

'Did you give him the wack [the share] then?' John wanted to know.

'Yeah.'

'That's nice. Most people would think that you wouldn't. How does it go? How do you cut it up?'

'Always equal shares.'

'Have you ever known anyone that doesn't?'

'No, never. You see the television and films, and you get Mr Big and it's laughable really. They go and get a hundred grand and bring it back to him and he gives them five grand each. Silly really. It's never like that. No Mr Bigs.'

Even when Derek was describing the most dangerous bank raids, he preferred to stress the fraternity rather than the competitiveness of it all, the mundane aspects rather than the sensational.

'Excitement?' he said, when I asked him. 'It never occurred to me. I suppose I could have got the money other ways. But to me it was just like going to work, but easier. I've been to work with people, you know, that like the excitement.'

'But did you take pleasure in it? I mean was there . . .?'

'There was no pleasure, no.'

'Well, was it a status thing? An ego thing? I mean did you look at other people who weren't prepared to take that kind of risk and think . . .?'

He was shaking his head as I was talking. Sitting across from me on the other divan. Medium height, sallow, matter of fact, domestic.

'No. I suppose, though, you could say it's a bit like a tightrope walker. A bit like that. You wouldn't get up there if you didn't think you were going to get to the other end, even though in your heart you know that one day you'll fall off.' He poured us some more Mateus as though mildly embarrassed by this flight of fancy.

'But why did you stick at it? You could have done something else, couldn't you?'

He thought about it for a minute.

'Well, the beauty of it is . . .' – I had a vague hope that we might be moving towards something just a shade more consonant with my dramatic theories – 'The beauty of it is, you can go and get it, and then go and have a holiday somewhere, and then, you know, come back. That lot's gone, but it doesn't matter cos you can go out and get some more, can't you? But, you know, with a weekly wage, it's just not possible, is it?'

Derek was matter of fact even about grassing. No, he couldn't recall any moments when he'd got near to doing it. He had no stories to tell of temptation resisted, or references to make to Koestler. I didn't need to press the point; John did it for me.

'Come on, Derek, why is there so much now? How d'you explain Leroy Davies, Germain, Smalls?'

'I think a lot of it is people who've done a lot of time. They can't face any more. A lot of them have been very successful: they've got a lot of money and don't want to lose it by going away. So when they get into their forties and the police threaten them with 15 years, 20 years or whatever, they just can't face it.'

But this wouldn't do for John. I wasn't the only person he'd spoken to at length about *omerta* – about that very special loyalty which robbers had to each other. And now here was one of those very beings suggesting that such an essential attribute could be subverted by what looked remarkably like a deterrent penal policy. Hand out 15 or 20 years for armed robbery and you'd have every villain in the business over 40 writing out a list of their accomplices and handing it to the nearest policeman.

'Yes, Derek. But why now more than before?'

'I think it started with the Richardsons [Charlie and Eddie]. They were grassed. And the Kray twins. And nothing was done to anybody. You know, like it's in the back of people's minds that nothing, nothing has happened to the people who grassed the Krays. And look who *they* are!'

Slowly, I was beginning to change my view of Derek. Perhaps the gradual darkening of the room was having something to do with it, but I now felt that there was a peculiar amorality about his view which perhaps made him even more frightening than the histrionic Phil. Even if Phil was a bit of a bully and a braggart, he didn't speak about hurting other people in the sort of tones that you might normally reserve for changing a washer on the tap.

'You see, John, years ago, if you was a grass, you got cut. And that was good. Cos you knew who was a grass. Most of the people with big cuts on their faces you knew were grasses. You didn't work with them. That's the trouble today. People's morals have changed. No grass has been hurt enough.'

I decided to pursue Derek's remarkably cavalier view of 'cutting' people, by asking him how he felt about all the other violence of his trade. He looked surprised that I'd mentioned it.

'More people used to get hurt years ago. When the police were less active. For a start, you'd be working eight-handed, instead of four or five as nowadays, and it was a cosh game. Hitting people over the head to make them behave. And as it was coshes, the other side would be prepared to have a go – perhaps even carry their own coshes to retaliate with. That meant a stand-up row in which people got battered.

'See, if a firm sent wages-clerks to collect wages, they'd get a couple of beefy boys from the warehouse to go with them as minders. They might have given them a couple of extra quid and I suppose they'd be thinking 'This is handy' – until someone coshed 'em. And you had to do 'em because it never did any good just threatening them, like, saying "Give us the fucking money." Cos they wouldn't hand it over. When we started using guns, though, we used to give them the orders to hand over the money and they did. Oh yes, violence has got much less since we started using guns.'

'Really?' I managed.

'Oh yes. When it's guns, you might only be firing rice or budgie seed, but it still makes a bang and brings a few lights down; has an effect. One shot in the ceiling, everyone hits the floor, and you can just jump over the counter and empty the tills.'

Although Derek's way of talking flattened out the violence, or threat of violence, involved in any robbery, this wasn't the first time I'd heard about the peculiar dialectic between banking-practices and armed robbery. In most cases it was the villains who led the way. Once guns became a regular feature of the bank raids, allowing a gang to terrorize the bank staff into such a state of submission that the money could simply be taken from the tills, something had to be done to block the way. In the late sixties, the banks, amid much clamour about the loss of personal contact with the customers, put up screens along the counters.

'What did you do then?' I wanted to know.

'Then you went through the doors; they'd have a side-door inside leading to the back, so you just, with a sledgehammer, smashed the door straight in. But then they got clever to that and had doors which opened outwards only, so you couldn't smash them in.'

'So then?'

'Well you switch to the next opening don't you. The outside window. On the wall behind the screen. In through there. And then out again. And what was good was that now they'd put the screen up, they'd put money back in the tills again. About eight grand minimum, wasn't it John?'

'But presumably they've now blocked up the windows?'

'Oh yeah. But as they made things too hard in the banks, we went to the vans instead. Guards were coming in delivering a hundred grand – across the pavement – in four lifts.'

Professionals now shy away from bank robberies, leaving the market to people Derek would call nutters, and John cowboys – dangerous amateurs who impulsively rush in demanding money and firing guns in all directions. 'They kill people,' said Derek simply.

Armed robbers have moved either to inside work – getting employees to provide special information on deliveries, or how to get out-of-hours access to safe-deposit boxes – or they have gone back down the line to moving security vans. These at least concentrate the money for the robber. According to Derek, they have one other advantage: 'Security people are much better: it's not their money. So you don't find them trying to be fucking heroes like the shop-owner who used to bring along his own wedge of notes.'

How ridiculous of the shop-owner to be a fucking hero and try to keep his money. It was something beyond Derek's comprehension; another of those trying aspects of the job which had to be overcome as best you could.

The sound of the television was now drifting into our little spare-room from the lounge, and Derek's wife came in with tea and Walnut Whips. It was dark enough for her to ask if we wanted the light switched on. No, we didn't. Grey seemed to be the right colour.

'Why d'you give up, Derek?' It was my standard closing question, even to those I suspected were still hard at some kind of villainy; a way of reminding them that they'd said nothing about their present activities. John hated the question. It always suggested reformation to him.

Derek was predictably undramatic. 'It became just another thing. Just like, well, tomorrow we're going to do that. And just go and do it. I used to stop and think about that, you know. I don't know if you know Billy Chester.'

John nodded through the gloom.

'He got shot you know.'

Another nod.

'I remember him saying to me one day, he said, like, as we were going to work, all tooled up, he said, "We're doing this as though we're going about a legitimate job. Going to the office. Matter of fact." And we were.'

Although John might have wanted some antidote to Phil's over-romanticism, I knew as he drove me at an unusually sedate 50 to 60 m.p.h. back across London that he could never go along with Derek's jobbing attitude. How could he admit that most of his own adult life had been spent paying the price for pursuing a way of life which could degenerate into such banality?

For John and for Phil, the sense of the extraordinariness of what they had been doing was essential. Derek's flat amorality – his casual sense that split heads were neither good nor bad – was incompatible with this belief. Phil and John and other robbers like them weren't just working for cash: they were fighting authority. Not in any genuine revolutionary sense – but as a way of asserting themselves against some notional system. They had no alternative but to break the rules: this was how they came to be themselves.

'What did *you* like best about it, John?' I'd pressed the question at him as we were coming to the end of our long session with Phil, the week before.

'Well it wasn't the money, Laurie. Not money. I'll tell you, I used to get a kick . . . especially when I was on the run . . . I used to get a buzz out of being wanted and outwitting them. Being around and surviving – not hiding like an animal in hibernation, but going out on the pavement and making out. I didn't feel superior, but I was playing another game to the one I presented. And most people are not playing another game. What you see is what they are; they're living the same lives as you see. The real criminal isn't: he's play-acting for most people, because his real life, what he really is, is hidden from most people.'

Phil had taken up the thread. 'Ah yes. Like when I was in

Marbella with my normal girlfriend and my normal friends. All normal. And none of them knew. Not one. It's like Clark Kent, isn't it? Glasses off and all that.' He laughed nostalgically, and went on.

'Oh yes. Nobody know, you know. It's like Zorro. He does it, then he totally disappears. Then it's all speculation. People sitting around everywhere. They catch a glimpse and say. "Look! Look! That was a bank robber." And then he's gone. And the bank robber can say to himself. "Yeah that was *me*, but you don't know that." That's why bank robbers all read the papers the next day. They have to make sure it was them. You can guarantee a lot who get arrested still have their Press clippings all folded up at home.'

He was still talking as he led John and myself down the hallway, along the wall-to-wall lime-green carpet. 'D'you know?' he said as he undid the double Chubb to let us out. 'I'm so fucking bored. Miss it all. I went out only last week to see the bank manager about some money I wanted for an investment. There I was, asking him nice and politely. And I suddenly thought: *Fuck me. Two years ago I would have jumped over the counter and helped myself.*'

5

Hoisting and Tweedling

In which the author meets Crazy Man — Harrods window is cleared out — and some jars are successfully tweedled.

In the middle of Derek's casual amoral chat about the need to cut grasses and fire guns to scare off 'heroes', there came a most peculiar admission. Something which sounded at first like an ethical reservation. I'd asked him if there was anything that he wouldn't do: any sort of professional villainy that he drew the line at. I suppose I thought he might mention being a gangster. Even for Derek, that might involve a little too high a disregard of normal human values. But his reply amazed me:

'Hoisting. I just couldn't do it. I don't know what it is.'

Did he mean that, being a big-time armed robber, he'd just find it too demeaning to wander around Selfridges stuffing jumpers under his coat? Was it the embarrassment?

'No. That's not it. No, I just couldn't do it. I mean just going in there.' He stopped to find an exact phrase to fix his antipathy. 'I'll tell you what. *It's too blatant for my liking.*'

But how could anything be much more blatant than his own game of rushing into a bank, firing into the ceiling, vaulting over the counter and rifling the till. 'You're joking, aren't you, Derek?'

'No. They are blatant. I mean armed robbery — you got surprise, ain'tya? 15 to 20 seconds, and you're in and out. And you've changed over cars before the call's gone through. To me it's that simple. But they're brilliant. They go in *anywhere*. I mean that fellow 'Dodger' was round here last week.' ('Not the Artful Dodger?' was on my tongue, but John's face wiped it off.)

'And he says: "Come on, we're going down Harrods. I'm getting some gear." And I went down with him, although I don't want to because I know what's happening. And then he says, "Well, what d'you want?" Well I don't want anything, do I?'

No, you couldn't imagine that Derek did want anything. He'd had many thousands of pounds from his robberies over the years and yet the council flat he now occupied had nothing to show for it. All the money had gone, without a moment's regret, on gambling and holidays.

'So I said, "Well, a tie, you know, like I don't wear ties. But it's true enough I've never had a tie. So I suppose I want one." But really I chose something simple like a tie cos I could imagine him taking a whole row of fucking mohair suits or something like that. And they'd be after yer an' all that.'

It had been already getting dark and quite difficult to see Derek's face looking back at us from the opposite divan, but there was enough light to catch his anguished mime: head darting to left and right in search of suspicious policemen, and arms laden down with imaginary mohair suits. The simple armed robber overwhelmed by the blatant hoister.

'"So," I said. "Look, just a tie. That's all I want. A tie." And we walked in, and the ties are all there aren't they? On the rack. And he goes "Right – which one d'you like?" And I'm sweating. So I say, "Oh – any one." You know, I couldn't be further away from it. "Well, mind my back," he says and swings me behind him. And then somehow he just went *whoosh* and they're all at one end of the rack – *whoosh* they're off – and then *whoosh* out of the door. The fucking lot. To him, it's nothing.'

Professional hoisters, I learnt, never took a couple of ties: they took the whole rack. The image that kept cropping up as I talked to other hoisters was always that of a plague of locusts: a team of professional workers who swept across whole counters and displays and took the lot. Cars with capacious boots, vans, and even small lorries would tour up and down the shopping streets of London, driving off from time to time for a rendezvous with a gang in a car-park, or to unload and come back for more. It was systematic looting which required a great deal of organization.

The first person into the store had the job of setting up the goods: perhaps putting a small elastic band around the ends of a few dozen silk scarves, or moving valuable bits of jewellery, or leather handbags, nearer the edge of the counters, sliding cashmere sweaters down the rail into a compact bunch. Then, if an assistant is around, he'll be engaged in conversation as far away as possible from the action, while a third member lifts the goods. If the walk to the door of the store is a little long, then there may be someone else to take over for the last stretch. No one is in possession for more than a few seconds, and it's always someone's job to obstruct anyone who seems to be getting too near the carrier. Rather like watching the Harlem Globe-Trotters in action: the loot works its way down from one end of the pitch to the other, but everyone involved seems to be able to display a clean pair of hands. Store detectives who move forward with well-founded suspicions may still find themselves clutching empty air.

Like con men, hoisters rely a great deal on distraction and sleight of hand, but they also depend on the sort of surprise element which gives bank robbers their advantage. They typically swoop on stores at times when attention may be slack – late afternoon is often favoured. One store detective I spoke to in Oxford Street told me that a professional could be in and out in half a minute. 'At any moment you might actually have two or three in the store mixed up with the customers. And then they start their moves. One walks this way. One walks another. And in between all that, out goes another five hundred quid's worth of gear.'

But, of course, there's always a couple of vital minutes during which one person is arranging the goods and another is waiting for the signal to move in. And because of the intrusion of shop assistants and customers, there inevitably has to be some loitering. Store detectives are trained to look for this moment; if they miss it they may well be too late. They're also looking for any contact at all between customers who otherwise show no sign of knowing each other, and for any displays of overfriendliness towards the sales staff.

Successful hoisters have long careers, but compared to some villainy it's hard work. After the silk scarves or cashmere sweaters or crocodile belts or leather handbags have been nicked, they've got to be sold, and hoisters often run a special risk because the lack of a chance to sell immediately means they have to carry stolen gear in vehicles and store it in lock-up garages or other 'safe' places. It's not unusual to hear stories of villains who've simply given up and taken enough of the gear home to allow reporters to greet the court case with yet another headline about 'Aladdin's Cave'.

I wanted to meet a top hoister. The couple of professional shop-lifters I'd chatted with at the Landsdowne kept telling me of other people I should talk to, but John seemed to take so little interest in any fresh interviews that I'd virtually given up hope. We'd apparently moved on to a new stage in our relationship since the interviews with the robbers, although I wasn't for the life of me quite sure what it was. At first it had seemed like progress: as though the suspended sentence imposed for fatuousness and silly questions had been lifted. We actually chatted about this and that, watched some football together on television (although I backed away from an argument over Hoddle), and, the most encouraging sign of all given his fundamental views on the proper strength for tea, he'd actually accepted without demur two cups of tea from pots that I'd made.

But, as the days went by, I began to suspect the reason for this new amiability on his part. For although he still went to the backroom in my flat where he usually worked on the book, I no longer heard the sound of the typewriter.

Occasionally I told him about my own progress: yawning, stretching my arms languidly, and saying something like 'Well, it's nice to have transcribed two sides of Phil's cassette.' But as nothing much more came back than a wan smile, I didn't feel able to go on to more specific matters, like asking for his comments on some ideas developed by Werner J. Einstadter of Eastern Michigan University in an article called 'The Social Organization of Armed Robbery'. Einstadter had interviewed 25 convicted robbers in California about how they viewed their activity compared to that of con men, and found that some spoke of it as more honest. Einstadter argued that

> Robbery is an open, direct, face-to-face encounter coupled with a non-disguised coercive demand: there is no stealth and furtiveness ... but a confrontation of unabashed power. It is this quality of candour that the robber equates with honesty, an apologia which ... makes the robbery career an object of worth, if not noble.

What did John think of *that*? Was it a way of understanding the status that robbery enjoyed among other professional criminals?

I never did get an opinion on Einstadter's thesis, but fortunately the hoister business was almost accidentally settled just a couple of nights later when John and I were having an early evening drink in the French pub in Soho. This was my choice as a place to meet rather than John's; just up Dean Street from Shaftesbury Avenue and not really a haunt of professional criminals. In fact, I'd been going there for years in the hope of running into some of the famous writers and artists who, according to the *Alternative Guide to London*, were supposed to meet there to exchange creative ideas.

'This is Tommy,' said John suddenly, as someone joined us at the bar. It was difficult enough to talk in the crush, let alone shake hands, but I nodded enthusiastically. 'Hoister,' said John, in a voice which announced: 'Well, it's what you wanted isn't it? Don't say I didn't do my bit.'

'Tommy. Tell Laurie here about going "half-way".' This was the contract work I'd heard about. There was no chance to switch on the cassette, so I tried hard to memorize the details while John ordered more Pernod.

Tommy did his best to oblige, explaining that 'half-way' in the hoisting game meant waiting till you were approached by someone who was moving into a new flat and wanted it fitted out. This customer would already have been round the main stores – Harrods, Heals, Maples, and decided on the fittings that he wanted. He then paid exactly half the price for them when they came round in the back of Tommy's van. This, of course, meant that Tommy had to steal only specified items, and not those which were best placed to be lifted. But this seemed to appeal to his professional pride, and, of course, he was getting an excellent price. 'Half-way' may not sound a lot, but few fences would pay more than a third.

His accomplice on all these jobs was a professional hoister whose exploits had earned him the name 'Crazy Man'. The dafter and more outrageous the commission was, the more Crazy Man liked it. That meant such things as manhandling large pieces of furniture straight down the main stairs of Maples (stopping on one occasion to ask the store detective the time), and then carrying them across the ground floor of the store and out of the side-entrance into a waiting van.

Unfortunately, though, it was becoming clear that any more news about Crazy Man was going to get lost in the general noise. I don't know any pub in the country which gets so crowded as the French. Sometimes you can wander down a virtually empty Dean Street, casually pull open one of the two doors which lead into the long thin bar and people *fall out*.

It was getting a bit like that now, and I managed to engineer a move round the corner into Old Compton Street and the Swiss, where, despite the usual collection of Kings and Queens of pornoland, it was at least empty enough to find a seat, and for me to get out the recorder. We might also be in for a more excitable interview that had been planned: the very nasty smell which hung around the bar suggested that someone had been freshening up with amyl nitrate. We got onto Harrods straightaway. All conversations with hoisters seem to head for that part of Knightsbridge.

'There was this once,' said Tommy. 'We'd just had this cutlery service away. Right from the middle of the display. And we was going back for more when Crazy Man suddenly sees this window. I couldn't believe my eyes. There they were. Five dummies all with white fur coats. Not mink. More expensive than mink. You know, the fur with spots down near the bottom of it. Anyway, the cheapest was sixteen grand. That was the cheapest. And that wasn't the end of it. All around these dummies was Regency silver gear. All perfect. Trays of it.'

Crazy Man had made some pretty blatant moves before, often helped by the large wardrobe of store coats which he possessed: all individually tailored and with household names lettered across the back of them: Maples, Selfridges, Heals. But even with his special Harrods: Electrician jacket, this was going to be a little more crazy than usual. Robbing one of the most stared-at windows in central London in broad neon-light. There was no way in through the door which led to the window inside the shop. But behind an advertising blackboard which was placed to the side of the door was a large panel on which Crazy Man got to work, while Tommy strolled up and down nearby keeping a look-out for curious passers-by or store detectives.

Tommy had the worst of it. Terrible noises came from behind the board as Crazy Man belaboured the old mahogany with a heavy chisel. Each crack seemed enough to arouse the entire ground-floor staff. But at least when the panel came away, they knew there were no further obstacles to getting into the window. They'd carefully watched while an assistant went in to touch up the display and had noted with satisfaction that there was no alarm bell.

Crazy Man slid through the gap and straight into his first public appearance in a Knightsbridge window. Tommy now had to work the other side, had to effect a manic air which would quickly repel anyone who advanced upon the window for an eyeful of the fur and silver. He successfully terrified a couple of tourists and glanced around to see how Crazy Man was doing.

'*Fucking hell!* There he was standing in the middle of the window. *Smoking.* Fag stuck in his mouth. A hundred a day he got through. One out and another one lit. But in the middle of the window.'

Tommy wildly distracted a few more sightseers and turned back to the window. What the hell was Crazy Man doing now? Why weren't the fur coats off the dummies? Well, he'd pulled at them hard enough, but they were all held in place by dozens of nylon wires – invisible to mere spectators – which helped to maintain their shape and style. And Crazy Man was now systematically burning through each nylon wire with the tip of his cigarette. One by one.

Finally, as Tommy went into an epileptic routine to distract a few more window-shoppers, Crazy Man broke the last wire, took out six dustbin bags from under his trousers, packed them full of coats and silver, backed out of the window and, looking smart in his Harrods jacket, stepped out into Knightsbridge to join Tommy for the quick drive home.

'He still had the same fag stuck in his mouth,' said Tommy admiringly.

Although even Tommy was still obviously amazed enough by this sort of outrageous behaviour to select it as a story worth repeating, what baffled him about his more everyday hoisting was why other villians weren't at it. It was all so easy. The shops were full of removable loot: just lying on the counter waiting to be nicked, and while you were thinking about your next move, you could always keep busy by collecting up a few of the cheque books, cards, wallets and purses which were lying around. All the new technology – television cameras, two-way mirrors, security tabs which trigger doorway alarms – was only there for the deterrent effect it had on amateurs. Anyone who could work skilfully enough to mask their actions from a shop assistant, and work too fast to be spotted by a store detective, was hardly going to be caught full-frontal by a camera or a mirror.

Security tabs had certainly caused a bit of a problem at first, but Tommy had already found ways to beat them. He told me one method because he believed it was now so well known that everyone was wise to it. All you did was to get hold of a tab for yourself and then set up the moves in the usual way – but wait for a customer to make for the doorway. That was the moment to drop the spare tab in her shopping basket. Off she innocently went, through the doorway, and 'brrr', off went the alarm system. 'Just a moment, Madam.' All the assistants immediately leap forward and out behind the crowd goes the hoister and his gear. Like the poor TV camera, the system is not quite fast or bright enough: it doesn't know how to scream just a little bit louder to let its owners know there's been a second violation.

I'd asked John before about 'fences' – big-time dealers who perhaps exerted some Fagin-like control over the thieves with whom they dealt. He'd told me I was wasting my time. And Tommy confirmed that there were few all-purpose Mr Bigs. You sold stuff 'here and there'. Perhaps you took furs to one place and cashmere to another, but often you just let it be known around the spielers and clubs that you had some gear and the network took over. Professional criminals are no more likely to go shopping for their clothes than they are to pay tax. And there seemed to be quite enough of them to provide a ready market for the sort of silk and cashmere and leather accessories which were favourite with the hoisters – particularly if they carried an Yves St Laurent or Harrods label.

I never quite found out whether the popularity of these up-market labels was a way of crediting the quality of the product, or the skill of the hoister. There's an ambiguity about the villain's preference for what gets called 'cream gear'. On the one hand it obviously sets them apart from that despised lumpen proletariat whose alleged dependence on keg bitter, *Coronation Street* and the *News of the World* makes them mere pawns in the hands of people 'in the know' in business and government. But it does suggest a different sort of gullibility. Take the case of the watches: a Cartier watch may cost £1,000 to buy in the shops, but there is no way in which any self-respecting villain is going to go along with the idea that it's worth anything like that price. That's what mugs pay.

One solution to the problem is to treat the object with indifference. Geoff made certain when you called on him at tea-time that you knew it was Dom Perignon in the ice-bucket, but then it was liable to be poured into your glass with no greater degree of ceremony than you'd accord to a litre of Hirondelle in an Indian restaurant. And if you did have an expensive Cartier – and many had this or something similar – it was the fashion to wear it loosely around the wrist so that the gold stretch-strap flopped casually against the back of the hand rather than being drawn tight around the wrist.

A still more cynical view of such status possessions was taken by the robber Phil and by a gangster named Milo. Their

Cartier Tank watches, John informed me, were 'snide' – counterfeit: very clever copies, but recognizable by those in the know – which of course included a pretty hefty proportion of all the people they ever met. An extra little twist to this 'snide' play was that Geoff in the time I knew him was also heavily into a little deal which involved importing champagne in specially designed bottles (I think it was Sicily, but people only talked in whispers about it and clammed up when I got near) and then relabelling it as Dom Perignon. John assured me, however, that he'd never dream of ever drinking the stuff itself. There were limits.

Watches and jewellery were the big-money end of hoisting, and although Tommy could talk about the techniques, it wasn't his game. You couldn't just walk up to jewellers, he explained, and clean out a display-case like you could a rack of silk ties.

'Except when we used to do the smash-and-grab,' said John nostalgically, as though describing a childhood prank. (I was beginning to wonder if it had been a mistake to stay on Pernod for a whole evening.)

'I never read much about that now,' I ventured.

'It isn't done now. No.'

'What did you do? What was a smash-and-grab raid?'

'Well, we used to do Burlington Arcade. Used to drive straight down there doing windows all the way. We did about three or four at a time. We used to take some real liberties. I go down there now and look at the stuff . . . and it's amazing to me how it stays in the window and no one has it away.'

'Is there better security now?'

'Yes. They've got special clamps on shelves so you can't have those off. And the window has been fixed so as soon as it's broken, down comes the grill. And they put posts up – like they do round council estates – so that you can't drive down there on the pavement.' John's indignation at this new traffic restriction demanded at least a moment's silence before I pressed Tommy to tell me more about hoisting jewellery.

He explained that you needed to find an expert, someone from the Garden [Hatton] who could be taken along to have a look in the window at, say, the ring you fancied, and then who could go back home and knock up a perfect replica for you – a 'jar' – so-called because nine times out of ten the stone would be made from jargon, a derivative of the relatively valueless mineral, zircon.

Then it was back to the shop for 'the tweedle' – for the switch – when at some time during inspection of the real ring, the jar would be slipped in to take the place of the purloined reality. All the usual con business, involving carefully timed distractions, would be used, and the real ring might well be left behind in the shop somewhere – stuck under the counter with chewing gum – so that the people who'd worked the tweedle could walk out clean.

But villains who were 'at the jar' were now much more likely to be found operating among people rather less sophisticated than jewellers – tourists, foreign businessmen, and (a special favourite) publicans.

'What they do', Tommy told me, 'is that a couple go into the bar, say at lunchtime when it's fairly quiet, and have a quick look at this ring they've got. All very hush-hush, but so that the governor can get a glimpse of it. You know, making out it's maybe stolen and all that. Then they get chatting about this and that and become friendly. "What d'you think of this then?" says one of them, bringing out the ring. 'I don't know how much it's worth, I should think about a grand, but I'll tell you what – if your missus would fancy it, why not take it along and get it valued and I'll let you have it for a bit less.' Well, what could be fairer? Here are these nice new friends of his trusting him with a valuable ring. And what's more, when he gets it valued, it's worth two grand. It's the real thing. So back he comes and says, 'Well, yes, it's worth about a grand.' And so he settles up. It's far easier to work the tweedle in a crowded public bar than in a jeweller's shop, and very soon off scuttles the mug to hand over the 'diamond' to his wife, who's delighted with the prize, especially when she learns the real value.

There is a dreadful irony in the fact that the last laugh in all this may be on another professional criminal. Weeks after chatting to Tommy in the Swiss, I heard from Les about the sad case of Patrick. It was a favourite cautionary tale down at the Landsdowne.

Patrick was a top-class burglar: he worked with a little team around the big London hotels, some of whom, from what I could gather, spent the rest of their time as cleaners or porters or receptionists: well placed to provide valuable information on who left what in their rooms when they went out. Two years ago Patrick 'had it off' in a really big way. One of the biggest coups of his career. There it was in banner headlines the next morning. 'FAMOUS FILM STAR LOSES £600,000 OF JEWELLERY.' He almost got a round of applause when he came into the Landsdowne the next day.

But Patrick wasn't so pleased about it all. He rounded on Tommy who came across to get him a drink. 'Fucking 600 grand. I tell you, I've done her a good turn. And her husband. He's been busy. There was only 70 grand's worth of kosher gear. The rest was jars. You can't fucking trust anyone these days.'

6

USERS AND DEALERS

In which Moroccan holidays are arranged for non-smoking hippies – Ronnie Scott tells jokes – and the author learns about duty-free bargains in Bolivia.

Colin always tried to deal in 'kosher gear'. His years in prison, and days spent around drinking-clubs like the Landsdowne, made him happy to describe himself as a professional criminal, as one who was 'at the game'. But he always maintained that the character of the illegal loot in which he dealt gave him a slight ideological edge over the common hoister, burglar or thief. Colin sold drugs. But not just for profit.

'What you've got to understand, Laurie, is that I'm a "user".' The term was important to him. It set him apart from the other dealers.

He may be as commercial as the next seller: busy wrapping 'weights' and kilos of Moroccan yellow and Lebanese red in clingfilm; pronouncing on the relative purity of 'speed' and the likelihood of this or that gram of coke being pure Peruvian or cut with 'pharm' (pharmaceutical cocaine); cheerfully pulling in a grand a week tax free. But he still insists on sharing with the relics of the flower-and-bells movement a firm belief in the actual benevolence of his main commodity – marijuana. 'You see, I don't go along with those who tell you that it's not as bad as alcohol or tobacco. That's negative. I still believe it's positively good.'

John was looking thoroughly sceptical. For a change I wasn't the cause of his concern. He just didn't like it when any of his professional criminal friends turned the slightest bit mystical. He could allow that Colin's colonial background set him a little apart from the usual vulgar materialism of London villains. But there was a limit. 'What about the casualties?' he demanded. 'Those who smoke too much?'

'Well, John, I've seen characters who *eat* too much. But nobody calls them casualties. I think I'm a better person for having used dope for 22 years. I know I'm *positively* better for using dope.'

We had all got together at Ronnie Scott's. It wasn't the ideal place for an interview, but Colin was anxious to catch the evening's star attraction: Yusef Lateef. Fortunately, the first set still had to start, and the only other people in the place seemed rooted to their seats.

'I got started in Ketama.' John and I looked puzzled. 'You know, Ketama: about 150 kilometres from Tangiers. It's the only place they're allowed to grow it; but they mustn't export it. That was in the days when Moroccan was still good – before it got the "Made in Hong Kong" label. I could get you Moroccan now in London for £20 an ounce average. But then, it was quite something.'

He went into a flashback: 'The women beating the grass on sieves and the fine pollen falling through the stack of trays with different sieves so that the lowest tray had the finest pollen in it. That's zero-zero quality, John. Simply pick up the pollen and squeeze it like that – and you've got dope. It's as simple as that. I always used to get half a kilo of that for myself. And 20 kilos to sell.'

The idea of a kilo of dope seemed almost silly to me. Occasionally, at student parties, I had seen beads of the stuff no bigger than a finger-nail being treated with a reverence due to the Koh-i-noor diamond. But 20 kilos. 'Wasn't it risky to buy so much?' I asked. 'I mean, before you'd got it organized.'

'No, no. That's the point. That's the whole point. If they know you're big, then there's less chance of you being handed over. What you have to know about dope-dealing is that it's treacherous. It's almost impossible to be a big dealer for any length of time without the law being on to you.'

'But that's where you do a deal. You put up some "bodies" to them from time to time – say a couple of small-time buyers every fortnight and everybody's laughing. *Everybody*. It happens everywhere with dope-dealing. A few years ago, in London, you could be arrested with say three ounces of good Leb, find yourself charged with having one, and then find the other two being sold back to you three weeks later. The police called it recycling.'

A few days later down at the Landsdowne, John was to introduce me to Robert (another big dealer, but a slick fast-talking Londoner with no time for any mystical nonsense about the effects of dope). Robert had his own name for the sort of dealers Colin was now describing. '*Twenty-per-cent boys*. That's someone in India or Pakistan who gets 20 per cent of whatever you're putting together for delivering you to the Old Bill. So if you're in for ten grand, they can count on two. The Yanks put up the money. The majority of dealers are grasses as well. *And they don't think it's wrong*.' Robert clearly had difficulty in imagining a society built on such shaky ethical foundations, but kept philosophical about it all:

'Let's face it. If you're dealing like me, your name has to go in. I get bottled off occasionally. It's something I expect and have to live with. The thing is, to do business you have to be known, and drug people don't have any qualms about trading "bodies". You have to trust people who can't be trusted. It's fucking diabolical. But it's better than going to work.'

Colin, however, had at least developed some ways to beat the system in Morocco. 'You never buy straightaway. You walk into the Ketama hotel – it's the only hotel and almost the only real building in the place – and they're round you like flies. "You want to do business? Nice hash! Look!" Then a guy comes along who doesn't talk hash straight away. He says, "You come to see my family; meet my people, my children." Then you feel a lot better. These are important things to a Muslim. He's not likely to do you after that. And if he does, then at least I know where he lives, and I can go back and do him.'

Yusef Lateef had come on. A huge Buddha of a man who planted himself centre-stage and blew intensely for half an hour on tenor and then flute, with no more acknowledgement of the audience's presence than an occasional impassive two-handed salaam between numbers. Colin looked pretty reverent about it all. Lateef was obviously a believer in the alternative reality: a soulmate, whose driving music validated Colin's lifestyle. We waited for the set to finish before we spoke again.

'How did you get back with that sort of amount?' I wanted to know.

'Simple. Down the window of the van. Plenty of space down there. But it's a terribly old dodge. It's almost routine now for the customs officer to say: "Ah! Wind your window down, Sir, will you? So that we can get a good look at you. Sticking is it?"'

But it worked *once*, and that gave Colin enough money to start up his travel company – the key to his fortune. He got the idea from a man who ran a garage for English-speaking people in Tangiers. First of all, buy a couple of mini-buses, then advertise some adventure holidays in *Private Eye*. Once he had the tourists over there, he announced that there would be a day in Tangiers for the vehicles to be serviced for the return journey. It was an extremely thorough service.

'Twelve seats had to come out. You had to unbolt the front seats, and check them first. Then the side panels would come out. Then in went 150 kilos of good Moroccan, and back went the panels. They were welded back in, but we had the place where they were welded tucked behind the ash-trays. Then all the seats could come in again and they would be bolted down.'

In any high-profit game like this, there is always the problem of how many people need to know. The garage people, of course, had to be included; but as they had no idea of the street-prices Colin could get in London, this was no great cost. Ideally, he would have liked to keep the drivers innocent. It is not easy to look natural when customs men are only a few inches off finding £50,000-worth of dope and setting you up with a five-year prison sentence.

'But the drivers just had to know,' Colin explained. 'I needed their help, because I was very insistent, very insistent, that none of the passengers got busted for even a little bit of dope. I had big signs in the buses saying: "NO DRUGS" and "DO NOT SMOKE".'

That had John laughing: the idea of 20 long-haired hippies all mystical from their African trip, perched on top of 150 kilos of dope, and being told to sit up straight and behave themselves. Colin caught the mood.

'Oh yeah, it got worse than that. The tours never paid, you see. We had to pay for the passengers. Get people we knew to go on holiday, so that we could fill the buses. I'd have friends shrieking, "No, please. I don't want to go to Morocco again." If somebody saw us in *Private Eye* and rang up on the phone and said, "How much is it?" we'd say "How much have you got?" Just to load them up. Two buses: while one was going, one was coming back.'

What I wanted to know was how the market worked. It always surprises me that dope is so readily available to those who want it, and the price is so stable. It makes the sales organization of some other popular commodities – records or whisky, say – seem positively anarchic.

Colin drew me a chart on the back of 'Forthcoming Attractions at Ronnie's'.

'Well, let's say I bring in 100 kilos. Then I'd sell that usually to two dealers – 50 kilos each at £1,200 a kilo. My own profit on that – and remember it has to pay my partner and our expenses – is around £500 a kilo. We're getting 50 grand altogether. A lot of money. There is a lot of money in dope. These dealers will break it down again and sell it, I would say, to about five or six dealers, each in quantities of five or ten weights. [a "weight" is half a kilo; it used to be a pound, but dope has gone metric]. They would charge, at top, £1,700 per kilo, which would make them – what – about £2,500 each. The next line of dealers then break it up into ounce or four-ounce deals. They would sell it at between £70 to £80 an ounce. Then sometimes even those who buy ounces may sell half to friends: but not for profit. Though there is still some trade for those amounts in pubs – small deals, five pounds or so. Enough for a few roll-ups. And, of course, it's right down there at the bottom where you find most of the mugs who end up in court.'

Meanwhile, Ronnie Scott was well into his interval act: the same 35 jokes as usual, in the same exact order, delivered towards the same spot of the audience from the same half-concealed position behind the stage-right pillar. We waited until the Scunthorpe sequence was over:

'The night-life in Scunthorpe finishes in the afternoon. I asked a taxi driver to take me where the action was: he took me to a place where they were fishing illegally. . . . It was the sort of boarding-house where you wiped your feet on the way out. The landlady said, "I hope you've got a good memory for faces?" I said "Why?" She said, "There's no shaving-mirror." . . .'

I decided to give Colin's moralistic pretensions a prod. 'But suppose you could get a good deal in heroin – found a way of bringing it in. Wouldn't you take it?'

Colin was quick to bring some principles to bear on the issue. 'I've tried every pleasure-drug there is including heroin, but I have a kind of . . . I'm slightly against chemical products. Things produced unnaturally in the lab. Like heroin. Like acid. Like amyl. Like speed. Stuff made in kitchens.'

He savoured his back-to-nature pose for a moment and then, as we kept silent, got a bit more practical: 'Actually, I happened to meet someone in Cambridge last month who is chemically minded and he said, "I'm making some speed." I said, "Is it good?" He said, "Yes, try some." I did, and it was not just good, it was excellent. Pure. Absolutely pure. I showed it to someone else and he said, "Fuck. There are no impurities at all in this." So I sell it. My best customer is a guy who sells to a lot of Hell's Angels. So when I see them on the road, I always give them a wide berth.'

Oddly enough, Robert too, when I met him at the Landsdowne, tried to get some ideology into the business of drug-dealing. He had no long history of using drugs or fascination with the East. He was a hard criminal who had done his training in other fields, and only switched to drugs because of the profits. But there he was in the club, a fat diamond ring on his left hand (a jar said John afterwards), and a very large Bacardi in the other – protesting his public-spiritness:

'All I want to do is to make people happy, and at the same time make a few quid. That's illegal? *It's outrageous*. I mean cannabis is a weed. It's a weed, John. It's a natural substance that grows in the earth, and they won't allow us to use it.'

In the last five years, good old natural marijuana has, however, become the fish and chips of the dope trade. Cocaine is the caviare. Why bother carting heavy chunks of Pakistani black around the country when you can make ten times the profit on a little bag of coke?

Colin was happy to get involved, although he was wise to the way in which coke's attractiveness was enhanced by its up-market affiliations. 'It doesn't do much for me. People who rave about it are kidding themselves a bit. It's like caviare and Rolls Royces. Like perfume, a status thing. And that's what makes it an unscrupulous market, why different kinds of people get involved in selling it.'

John and I nodded and waited. Patiently. By now we seemed to have a tacit agreement that there'd be approximately twenty seconds silence whenever Colin stumbled over any more scruples, or got caught up in a cloud of nostalgia for the days when dealers thought more of their souls than their profit margin.

'It's so easy to fool people. All those rich people. Most of those who're chucking it up their nose, they're not chucking up coke; they're chucking up everything from Harpic to vitamin B. Apart from the people who free-base, who're so affluent that they can buy an ounce. Apart from them, everything gets cut. That's the wonder of hash.

'You can't pollute hash. But with coke it doesn't matter. There's a whole industry of cutting coke. You test people out. Sell them an ounce of pure coke, say. Then next time cut a bit. Not much. Now if you get caught out, you go, "Oh I'm sorry, I didn't mean," and then you go back to the other level. But if he doesn't detect the five per cent, it means he's lost the test. And then you can cut it a bit more for the next ounce – you call it "treading" – and go on and on. Tread it to death. Every dealer gets this knowledge. So all coke-dealing is crooked in that way. It's a con.'

Smuggling coke is also much easier than marijuana. Colin described one friend who had come up with a technique for mixing it up with distilled water. 'Coke mixed with distilled water looks just like white wine.'

'Doesn't it sediment?' asked John.

'No. Well, it does. But one quick shake. No sediment again. And you can work it through the duty-free. You see, duty-free goods are almost never checked. So one guy goes out. Buys the coke. Usually Bolivia is the cheapest and best. He mixes it with distilled water. Puts it into wine bottles, and corks and wraps them professionally. They then go into a duty-free bag which is resealed. Off he flies to an international airport, where he changes planes and meets another guy in the duty-free concourse, who puts the bottles in his own duty-free bag. Back comes the second man to London with two duty-free bottles of wine. The beauty of it is, he's never been near South America'.

By the end of the evening at Scott's, my head was buzzing with news of this and that deal – of the advantages of Bolivian coke – the fact that most of the highly prized Afghan came from Pakistan – that drug dogs couldn't smell cannabis if you kept it packed in clay – that most of the drugs in this country still arrived through embassy arrangements – that tabs of Operation Julie acid were now collector's items.

The music had finished some time ago and waitresses were sniping at us by noisily emptying ash-trays and moving chairs. In a minute or two they'd be asking us to lift our legs so they could vacuum under the table. Our almost empty bottle of Valpolicella looked a little mundane after the exotic pharmacology of the last few hours. I remembered a sad little story I'd once read in *Rolling Stone* which seemed to fit the mood. It would round off the evening with a laugh.

The author of the story, I explained, came from South Wales and back in the early fifties, he and his friend had been passionately interested in the Charlie Parker-Dizzy Gillespie bebop revolution which was taking place in New York. Not just the music, but the whole cultural style of the movement, and in particular the drug scene. For months they'd tried to find someone in Cardiff who could sell them some of this magical 'grass' they'd heard about which seemed able to make you play alto like 'Bird' and piano like Thelonius Monk. Eventually, a seaman sold them a little packet of the stuff. Now where would they go to smoke it? Romantically, they decided that they'd head for the hills and settle themselves down in a remote rural pub where no one would have the faintest notion that the stuff in their roll-up was a dangerous New York narcotic. Sitting at the bar-room table, they carefully got out their tiny pile of grass, placed it on one side, and then began to assemble the Rizlas. Almost immediately, the country yokel sitting next to them showed great interest. 'Here,' he said, sliding himself alongside them. 'Don't you know how to roll a cigarette?' And with that he picked up the Rizlas in his left hand, and with a casual sweep of the right sent the grass flying across the bar-room floor. 'Now, where's your tobacco?' he demanded.

'One thing you *can* say for Ronnie Scott,' said John, as we piled out into early morning Soho. 'At least his stories are short.'

7

CHAMPAGNE CHARLIE

*In which Mark defrauds a few bank managers – forgets his lines
– and goes stark raving mad.*

'It's ten-past twelve. I'm going to get raped tonight.'
'Who by?'
'The rapist. You know, in the papers.'
'He won't rape you. He only rapes people who live in
basement flats.'
'I live in a basement flat.'
'Boom. Boom.'
The gang of girls at the next table in the Bahamas cocktail
bar had all looked about 17 when they were sitting down. But
now that worries about the time had overtaken them, and
bags and coats were being scrambled together, there was the
unmistakeable sound of the fifth form leaving for home.

I looked across at John's Bacardi and Coke. It had probably
been a wiser choice than my own Homicide Rouge cocktail
('they could have used these on St Valentine's Day instead of
machine guns – £3.00,' said the menu), which had quite
enough Tia Maria in it to bring back memories of the worst
kind of Christmas past. I fiddled with the menu and
considered switching to Daquiri or even Godfather – 'so
called because it blows your head off' – on the next round.

I had another quick look around the basement. It had to be
quick. There were so many poseurs in this place, so many
people dressed up as hippies, punks, gangsters, romantic pop
stars, American soldiers, and rastafarians – all wanting a bit of
eye contact to guarantee their presence – that nice long looks
in any direction could quickly become meaningfully
entangled. Even people who looked as though they might be

what they looked like turned out not to be. Only minutes before I'd nodded towards a squat mesomorphic guy standing at the end of the bar under the huge Casablanca ceiling fan, and whispered 'Gangster?'

'No,' John whispered back, 'but *he* is,' pointing towards a glazed, long-haired youth in a group on my left who up till then had looked altogether more Haight Ashbury than Wormwood Scrubs.

I couldn't think why Mark wanted to meet us here. If he really was the international cosmopolitan fraudster John had claimed, then why weren't we tucked up in those big armchairs they have in the cocktail bar at the top of the Park Lane Hilton, rather than sitting on these little chairs round a raffia table in Notting Hill.

In fact Mark, when he did eventually arrive, looked more Notting Hill than Park Lane. About 40, neat spade beard, grey suit, college tie, a little overweight. Rather like a car-salesman I thought, but Porsches rather than Metros. His gestures were old-fashioned sharp; bird-like twists and turns of the head; sharp, pointed movements with the hands. 'All right, John? What's this you're drinking? *Bacardi and Coke?* What the fuck's happening to you. I don't know.' And when he walked to the bar to get his first bottle of St Emilion, he had a little bit of that style which James Booth perfected in British films – small, quite dandyish steps with the shoulders held back, arms loose at the sides and the hands moving slightly at the wrist as though touching away some troublesome undergrowth. Deep down in John's international fraudster there was still a spiv struggling to get out.

Nothing about his appearance prepared me for the flood of rhetoric which poured out as soon as he'd settled back into his chair for the interview. He'd been well briefed by John before – indeed, had only agreed to come because he owed John a favour – but his total frankness and sheer ebullience about his life was quite unexpected. All I said was something longwinded about nobody quite knowing what it was that got people into, well, you know, professional crime, and how did he, personally, himself, get, sort of, started.

'I tell you. I know the exact moment. The moment I saw two grand in readies for the first time in my fucking life. Pound notes. On a little deal. Nothing.'

He explained that in the late sixties he'd had a small nightclub in Streatham which various criminals patronized, and a little firm which had developed a clever line in fleecing casinos and gamblers had put him in a scheme.

'They put me in a deal and flew me to Bermuda. I got the punter on board to spend ten grand and they had all the coppers straightened out in Bermuda and it was all lovely. They got the money and I had to come straight back here. Well out of the way. So that the coppers, when they handled the guy, could blame it on me.'

I knew just enough about these 'sting' operations to follow the outline of the plot. But Mark was plunging on.

'Now, John, you know Pete and his people, well it was them, and they still saw me as a straight man . . . so, like they don't fancy giving me my corner. They came back from Bermuda and said: "Oh, it's all gone wrong. The Old Bill went crooked on us and we were lucky to get out of it without being nicked." I knew that the punter hadn't done anything more than wipe his mouth [accept the inevitable], but they were talking about other business and I didn't do anything.'

So there he was back in his nightclub, having been gently conned. He could have shrugged and just got on with normal life.

'It wasn't as though it was my dough they'd taken. But then I brooded and thought it *was* my dough and I thought, I want my money back. So I get on a plane, don't know quite what I'm doing, but I go and see Pete and Ronnie and I demanded my whack. Cos I knew it was a fucking take-on.

'And they gave me my money back in Marbella. Never forgot it. I thought, here I am, a nice straight guy – and they fucking gave it me back. That was the first time I started.'

I don't know whether Saul actually grinned at that moment on the road to Damascus, but if he did, he must have done so as delightedly as Mark did now. This was the conversion which transformed his life. It really was. He'd found his god.

'Oh, I loved it ... loved it. It was absolutely ... Words couldn't describe it ... yes, they could ... I thought, this is a piece of cake. All this fucking dough you could get. I don't wanna work 24 hours a day. There I was ducking and diving, wining and dining. Champagne fucking Charlie.'

(I remembered an American television programme I'd seen a few weeks before in which a group of surly youngsters who were reckoned to be potential delinquents were taken along to a state prison to be lectured by some tough-talking inmates on the perils of a life of crime. The expert who was rolled out at the end to comment reckoned that the idea worked very well: it made crime unattractive, put the kids off it. Just as long, that is, as they didn't run into Mark on the way home.)

'Well, I'm a natural,' he was now insisting, as John asked if he ever had any doubts. 'I mean I am a natural. I loved it. I loved the high life. Everywhere I went it was first class. Whenever I went to New York or Australia, it was first class. Three grand a trip. Tremendous.'

My next question was usually the moral one. 'Did you feel that you were doing wrong?' or 'Did you ever think about the victims?' or 'Did you feel guilty about what you were doing?' But it was difficult to see how I could launch any of these worthy vessels into this effervescent tide. I vaguely asked, 'Did it ever worry you at all? You know, what you were doing?' The answer came racing back.

'See, I'm a great believer in this,' he leaned across the raffia table to press the point, 'that in my life, whatever I've done, all I've ever done is banks, finance people and the rich. I've never fucked anybody else. People that can well afford it have been fucked. Right? And they're covered by an insurance company, so why the fucking hell are we talking about being worried? And...' a forefinger in front of his face emphasized that this was the point he wanted to press, 'and I've always done it – but lovely...' a broad smile, '... by the stroke of a pen. I've never hurt anybody. Right.' His glance between us sponged up more approval. 'And I've always drunk with bank managers. I've always said "Look, have a drink," before I nicked all the dough off them.'

Mark used up-market but trendy venues like Mirabelle's in Berkeley Square to wine and dine his various bank managers. (I asked naïvely how you managed to get a bank manager to dine with you, and he gently explained that 'You asked them.') He'd set them up one after another, often, because he enjoyed the joke, at the very same table, but always working under different names and with slightly different stories. What he had to do over the meal was lull them into a sense of false security, and then at the right moment lob in a bit of 'hard evidence' about, say, the success he'd just had in selling his own property for 43 grand and about having found another place to buy.

His next job is to pay in the moody cheque, made out, of course, to himself, or at least to the assumed name in which his account is held. He didn't want this to go through too quickly.

'So what I used to do was go up to Scotland. I used to go up to the Islands and pay it in there. Right? So I knew it takes – well, in the Isle of Skye if there's bad weather – it takes a long time to get the fucking cheque over to the shore. So by the time it gets to my bank, there's like ten days gone. Right. So I'd go up there, pay it in, and the credit transfer would go through.'

Then it was back to Mirabelle's with the man from

Barclays. 'I'd have another solicitor's letter typed and I'd say, "Oh, look. The deal's completed. The cheque's coming.' And he'd look at me as if he'd already got it in his bank. All that's left then is for Mark to pay in a cheque for, say, 25 grand, payable to an account which he holds in another name at another bank, and then to call in and draw out 20 grand of that in cash.

It is all, of course, an example of the exploitation of that psychological credit which invariably accompanies any system of financial credit. But whereas most of us have to resort to bridging loans to cover the hiatus between receiving payments and making them, Mark and other more genuinely creditable souls are able to use bridging rhetoric.

Not that it was always word-perfect. Every good actor fluffs the occasional line and I'd noticed that in most con men and fraudsters you'd find the equivalent – a moment when the whole elaborately conceived swindle was threatened by a negligent move or inappropriate remark. Sometimes, it seems that these miscues are almost subconsciously engineered as a test of improvisational skills, or perhaps to provide a delicious reminder of how thin is the ice upon which they skate. Mark was no exception:

'One time I was in Mirabelle's I'll never forget it, cos this time the cheque came to a balance of about 38 grand and I'd gone, "Oh, there's the solicitor's letter." Mark's voice dropped to a dramatic whisper. (Not too loud in case the bank manager could still hear.) 'And I'd forgotten to sign the fucking thing. Thank god, he'd had enough booze. He just went, "Oh, lovely." Just like that. With his fork. He went, "Oh, lovely." *Amazing*.'

Even though Geoff and Mark have very different games to play, they both thrive on alternating between the smooth casual conversations which set up the mark and the frenzied wheeling and dealing behind the scenes which is necessary to make that front possible. Geoff has his frantic milk run from bank to bank, and Mark the regular dash from the printers to an out of town bank and back again to the bank manager. It is really the implausibility of this quick-change routine, the transformation of a customer into a hustler in the space of a couple of minutes which makes managers and tellers susceptible. At the end of the whole elaborate charade, there is the denoument – the brief moment when after all the twists and turns and distractions and moody letters, some actual hard cash slides across the counter. Waiting for this final seal of approval upon your act can be the most difficult part of all to manage. Have they guessed? Are they waiting to nick me as I take the money? What are we waiting for? Is someone checking?'

'I sat in this bank manager's office once,' Mark recalled. 'Now, he thought I was from the Diamond Board, you know, in Hatton Garden. Sat in his office, and he said, "Well Mark." No, not Mark – whatever my other name was, David, Dick, Harry or George. "Have a drink." Out comes the bottle of sherry, and I promise you, we sat there, on my baby's life, for two fucking hours. Till about quarter to three in the afternoon. And I'm thinking, "Fucking hell! I hope everything's all right." I've drunk with him then till half-past three, till the bank's closed, then got up casually, gone to the counter, "Oh, have you got something for me?" and there it is in an envelope. And I walked out with it.'

Mark's celebration of his life of crime was doing a great deal to keep the Bahamas cocktail bar at bay. The stage army of bourgeois punks and mock gangsters and weekend rastafarians and elderly new romantics was quite put to rout by his cheerfully honest duplicity. Even the whirring Casablanca fans seemed less objectionable: Bogart might not have exactly hit it off with Mark, but he'd certainly have kept a table for him in the club.

Even more for Mark than for Geoff, this delight in story-telling is a form of practising, of keeping in trim for the next occasion when a credible story has to be conjured up to pay the rent. I'd sometimes wondered how much I was conned by these stories of other cons, but John's presence did much to ensure that people played it straight; in this relatively small world it was easy enough to find some confirmation if you felt suspicious.

It is, of course, exactly this sort of demand for confirmation which Mark could find himself facing if anything went wrong with the front he was presenting. There had to be some back-up to his act: it was no good if as soon as one string broke, the whole costume fell away. Unlike an actor, there was no way in which he could walk off stage if he fluffed a line – there's no dressing-room with a bottle of scotch for consolation, only a cell. Whatever the hand facing the professional fraudster, he must desperately reshuffle in an attempt to get himself back in the game. Mark had his Heathrow story as an example.

'I got to the airport and I'm going back to the States. Dud cheques, banker's drafts, moody passports. The lot. Got to Heathrow, and I walked in and, I don't know, but it was, you know, sort of off. Something wrong. I've got to customs and they've gone, "Oh yes. Now tell us where you think you're going."'

'I went, "Well I'm going back to the States."' Mark's voice moved up into executive overdrive, an impersonation which was so effortless and effective that you wondered why he didn't use it all the time: it seemed as much his voice as the other, much flatter London voice which he used alongside it.

'"You can see that can't you? From my papers. I'm going to the States." There was two of 'em and I knew . . . I said to myself, "Mark, you've got to pull it all out."'

As he explained to us, he'd handled this sort of scene hundreds of times before – with customs, police, bank managers, estate agents. But on this occasion the premonition he'd had suddenly started to interfere with his lines; he began to wobble on the tightrope.

'I went, "Anyway . . . er . . . where can I get . . . where can I get . . ."' Mark simulated his desperate spluttering for words, the con man without a proper sentence to his name. 'I don't know what happened to me. I fucking went to pieces. I went, "Where can I get a . . ." They said, "What do you want, Sir?" I went, "A drink . . . er . . . a Scotch . . . er . . . I'd like a . . . you know . . . a . . ." So I knew I'd ballsed it. For some reason I'd fucked it up.'

And he had. They sat him down and systematically began to go through his papers and belongings.

'I've just sat there and I've got the paper out and I was just reading but not reading, cos my mind was racing away like Ovett and Coe. As I read, Laurie, it was just like in a film. Every exit was covered by coppers. Suddenly every exit, all around me. So I still sat there and thought, "Fucking hell, I'm gone."

'After ten minutes, speakers in the airport . . . "Mr Drake. Mr Simpson." Or whatever my name was. I forget now. The plane was taking off. Fucking Boeing. Fucking first class. Up comes the stewardess. "Mr So-and-So," whatever my name was, "the plane is waiting for you." I said, "Look. OK, I'll be there. But you'll have to wait." I pointed out all the hoot around me. Held the whole fucking plane up. Speakers still going, "Mr So-and-So . . . last call." Stewardess waiting. And while this is happening, in they walked. Two jollies. Fraud squad merchants. Two of 'em. In they've come. They've gone, "Hello, Mark." Mark . . . Can you imagine what that did to me? Fucking Mark. I said, "I beg your pardon." Do you know what they did? Now, how they did this only you may know. I can tell you this on my life. They pulled a photograph out and showed it to me and said, "You are Mark Spedding." And I've looked at the photo and I promise you . . . it was me. I had on one of those coats . . . whatdcallit . . . er . . . you know . . . no sort of shoulders.'

John quickly supplied 'raglan'.

'That's them. And the dark bins on. Right? And as I've looked at myself, it's all gone into slow motion. But I know I've got to say something. And I went, "God, now I realize why all this is going on."' Mark's overdrive voice was charged with mock relief. 'I've gone. "Ah, now I can see why you've held me up. God, why didn't you tell me?" And suddenly I know I'm back on form. And I'm playing "mystery solved" and "what a big joke" and "now I understand". And they've looked and their faces are like that. Mark's face came over insecure. 'I've got 'em on the run. I know. And I'm laughing away. Laughing to myself, *and* as part of the business. "Oh dear . . . ha, ha . . . doesn't he look like me? It could be a twin of mine. But I'd never wear that dreadful overcoat." I promise you, John, it was unbelievable.'

Like every good con man though, the fact of being on thicker ice made him pile on even more weight. His delight at regaining mastery of the situation led him into one of those superfluous flourishes which con men and other villains seem to relish as marks of their superiority.

'Now this is where I nearly put myself right back in it. I'm using my head, and the brain is going like this.' He whirled a finger by his temple. 'And they said, "Well, what do you do?" I've gone, "Actually, I'm a property dealer but" – and this is where I've gone too strong – "but I'm also training to be a barrister." I've always fancied I'd be an incredible barrister and you know how coppers call people like that "Sir". So it was "barrister". They said, impressed, "Oh!" and I can't leave it alone and I've said, "At the LSE." The silly cunts stood for it. I didn't even know if they do law at the LS fucking E. How the fuck would I know? But they never chased it. They went, "Oh, all right then." Cor, it was all right and all. I promise you I walked away. And I made the champagne on the plane.'

It was easy to see that Mark's exuberance was doing more than pushing the decor of the Bahamas into the background. John had been smiling and laughing along with the stories, and had even at a couple of points given me the sort of collaborative look which said: 'There I told you he'd be good value, didn't I?' I knew by now that he'd stopped writing shortly after the meetings with his fellow armed robbers: Derek and Phil. I guessed that it was a combination of feelings. There was the usual dissatisfaction with my questions, especially when, as in that case, they'd been blundering about in an area he knew so well, but also a sense that he had a deal more in common with Derek and Phil than he'd originally expected. He couldn't 'sell them out' without also selling himself. Much of his identity was still based on a belief in many of the criminal values which Derek and Phil and Mark and Geoff articulated. It was part of him – a substratum of his personality – which couldn't simply be removed and placed on one side for casual inspection by outsiders. Those values provided him with his sense of difference from the rest of the world. It wasn't, though, something that I could exactly discuss with him. My references to relationships between his identity and his criminal allegiances could only come out as patronizing. I would sound like a social worker nudging along a group therapy session.

Although Mark made no eventual difference to John's decision to back away from the project, he did provide for at least one evening, a vivid demonstration of how an obviously intelligent and sensitive human being could become so caught up in villainy that he stayed with it all his life. Mark's initiation into crime may have depended upon that 'pile of dough' he was able to collect in Marbella, but it was obvious that it was not money which remained the driving force so much as the sheer excitement of not being firmly fixed within the world, the thrill of being always on the edge.

There was nothing at all pathetic about Mark, none of the half-excuses and quarter-regrets which run through so much of the biographical and auto-biographical material on professional crime. There was no reference to difficult childhood, or villainous companions, or the oppression of authority. It reminded me of a story John had once told of a lecture he'd given to a large audience of probation officers somewhere in the north-west. At the end of the talk, one of them stood up and congratulated him on his book (*McVicar by himself*). This, he said, he had found to be very moving. It had greatly helped him to understand why John became involved in crime, and the struggle to overcome his criminal predilections. However, he had detected in his film a much cruder approach. In the film he merely seemed to be enjoying himself when he was out robbing banks and on the run. How could he explain the difference? Was the film untrue?

'Well,' John had replied, not, I suspect, without a certain enjoyment. 'That's exactly as it should have been. Because, you see, the book with all its accounts of childhood and causes was written originally as my defence statement, when I'd been picked up again after the escape. It was really written for people like probation officers. So I'm glad you liked it. The film, on the other hand, was a bit more about how it really was.'

I think he swallowed quite a few reservations about the film to make his point – but it was true enough in its way. Years before, when I'd produced a glowing review of the book for *New Society*, he'd written from prison to say, 'I'm surprised you were so impressed by what you must know is what other cons would call a "sad story".'

Maybe no glimpses of this sort of 'sadness' intruded upon Mark's story because he had never spent more than a few weeks inside. Not that he'd managed this without some effort. For whenever prison looked inevitable, he'd acted his way out of trouble, using all his professional gifts of mimicry and duplicity to convince judges, policemen, doctors and warders that he was completely and utterly mad. It would start as soon as he was remanded in prison.

'They'd say, "What's your name?" I'd go, "What d'you want to know for?" And I'd fold my arms and look at them all nutty, you know. And then I'd rub, rub, rub, until I'd rubbed all the skin off.' He rubbed his wrist vigorously against the raffia table. 'I'd bleed in the end. Then I'd try to get out through the bars. And they'd say, "This one is fucking loony."

'Of course, all I wanted was to get up in the dormitory with the other nuts and have a telly and put my feet up. The first time I was really frightened. I'd always been terrified of going to prison. I thought, I've got to get out. "Mark," I told myself. "You've gotta get yourself put in a hospital."'

The person he had to convince was the Home Office doctor.

'I said, "And who are you?" He said, "I am So-and-So, the Home Office doctor." I said, "How do I know? You haven't got one of those things round your neck." Straight away I knew I had him cos of how eager he was to show me he had one. He's going, "It's in here. I don't use it today." I said, as if I'd caught him out, "Show it to me. Show it to me." He went, 'It's here. Calm down. It's in here." He opened a drawer and brought a stethoscope out. I completely ignored it. I told him that the FBI and the CIA had followed me when I was in America. He asked me how I knew. I said, "How do I know?" Like he had to be crazy to ask. I stood up and pulled my shirt up and pointed to my appendix scar. I went, "Look, see that. You think I don't know they're fucking after me. They put a radio transmitter in there. You think I don't know?"' Mark was jabbing his stomach to emphasize the point; his voice was having to ride through yelps of laughter from John.

'On my life. On my life. He's gone, "Settle down." I've gone into him now. He'd been having it easy up to then. I've gone, "Anyway, you're not a doctor. You're FBI. I know you are. I don't want to talk to you." And by now I'm up and about, looking all agitated. And you know what he's done? He's shouted for a screw. He's gone, "Officer! Officer! Take him away." And as the screw is taking me back to my cell, he's saying to another screw, "He really is a fucking lunatic this one. He's stone raving mad." I'm going to myself, "Thank fuck for that." Got back in my cell and it was like ecstasy.'

Unlike his other cons this one had to be kept up for nearly every minute of every day. 'Wouldn't eat. I banged the doors all night and day. They nearly put me in a padded cell. They're coming into shoot me through the fucking windows. Bang. Bang. Everything. The works. I pulled it all – every day, every night. Cos I thought I gotta win. I've gotta win. Right? It really . . . what's the word? Drained me. It was really draining. It got so I wasn't sure if I was going mad. It's like doing that *Over the Cuckoo's Nest* thing.'

Of course, the police who arrested him and saw him pull all his other routines weren't likely to be convinced by the sudden emergence of this paranoid schizophrenic. But they were so entertained by it that they were happy to let it go. It wasn't them who were being conned any longer. It was everyone else.

'At the death, at the death, I'd done such a fantastic act in the court, in the Bailey, I had everyone at it. I was saying to the screws under the Bailey, "I've gotta have tablets." They'd bring 'em. Getting doctors down. Driving the judge mad. Sacking me counsel saying he was in the plot to get me. And all the coppers down there." Mark briefly gestured to indicate the well of the court. 'Sat there, listening, looking up and laughing at me. Honestly, you could see they was trying to keep a straight face . . . The Chief Inspector met me to pick up a few quid I had for him after I came home. He said, '*Mark. Fucking unbelievable.*' Said he couldn't stop laughing. Said I was so good I deserved to get out of it.'

And he did – Mark went straight from court, not to prison, but to a private sanitorium. Another man might have decided that now was the time to give it a rest, but a professional criminal can't look a gift alibi in the mouth.

'I was never there. Never there. I was grafting every day. I was getting on the train every day and coming back to London. Doing frauds and banks, then running back to the hospital for cover. One time in London when I was doing it, I went and nicked a couple of grand from a bank. The coppers came round to the hospital. I screamed, "Nurse! Nurse!" The nurses came out, and I said they were persecuting me. The nurses ordered them out. They said, "Never fucking mind 'out'. He's been in London and nicked two grand out of a bank."'

Mark finished his St Emilion, and John, despite some heckling, stuck to Bacardi and Coke, while I had another Homicide Rouge. They seemed to grow on you. On the way out, at the bottom of the stairs, I came across a lighting display I hadn't seen before. Against a glowing pink neon backround, a green-sprouted golden pineapple was rising from the sea like the morning sun. It really did look rather nice.

8

WE ARE THE POLICE

In which the author learns how to do a deal – cop a plea – duck his nut – and, finally, discovers an honest policeman.

I'd realized by now that I was going to have to wait for John to come to me. My eager, early-morning telephone calls asking about the time and place for our meeting with the burglar he'd promised to deliver, were a thing of the past. As I could hardly go out and find my own professional criminals and fix up an interview, there was little else to do but sit back and hope that the peculiar 'will I, won't I' that John now seemed to be dancing with his former villainous friends and acquaintances would soon be resolved in my favour.

I decided to fill in my spare hours by talking to those various writers, journalists, and researchers from Fleet Street and television who at one time or another had made professional crime their special area. As the evenings had to be kept free for possible calls from John, that meant a lot of lunches: fish and chips in a café off Fleet Street with John Ball from the *Sunday Times* Insight team and co-author of *Cops and Robbers*; veal escalope in the executive canteen on top of Thames TV with producer Jerry Gable; spartan vegetarian lunch at the Battersea flat with Gordon Newman, author of the *Law and Order* TV series.

Much of what they had to say about run-of-the-mill villains confirmed my own material, but I did find that their knowledge of professional crime was particularly encyclopaedic in an area that I'd so far neglected. In fact, several of them, notably Martin Short, co-author of *The Fall of Scotland Yard*, and Peter Chippindale, the ex-*Guardian* reporter, suggested that I'd be unlikely to find any other group of offenders whose financial run of success and compulsive recidivism so well qualified them for inclusion.

It was this insistence which led me to risk a night off from telephone watching and took me down to the Albion in Ludgate Circus. When I arrived, there were no more than half a dozen people in the entire place, and most of them looked as though they'd strolled in accidentally and would be on their way to a livelier setting once they were through with their half-pints. Fortunately, I wasn't there for a social evening or a liaison: I wanted to look for myself at the scene of a bizarre incident which I'd been told had happened in this very saloon just three years before.

It had then been a similarly quiet evening, with so few customers in fact that the publican's wife had had plenty of time to observe the two distinguished-looking gentlemen who were drinking at the bar. They were eagerly exchanging details about meeting-places and money and nodding in agreement. Probably a business deal being sorted out.

She cleared the bar of a few empty glasses, and looked up again to see the two men nodding together in satisfaction. The older man put his arm round his companion's shoulder and gave him an affectionate hug. That was the moment when everything started to go wrong.

Instead of the older man dropping his hand to his side after a brief embrace, he started squeezing harder and harder – almost as though he was trying to crush the younger man. Voices were raised.

'You bastard.'

'You give me that.'

'I will not.'

Suddenly they were at each other: the older man lunging forward to grab at his companion's coat. They fell to the floor, scuffling wildly. Other customers scattered in fright. Only the publican's wife stood her ground.

'*Right*,' she said, leaning over the bar to glare at the tussling duo on the floor. '*Right*. If you two don't stop now, I'll call the police. I'll call the police.'

Slowly the struggling stopped: the younger man disengaged himself, pulled his face above the bar, and hissed indignantly: '*We are the police*.'

In fact, not *just* the police – but very high-ranking officers: Detective Superintendent John Keane and Detective Inspector Bernard Gent. And the fight had been set off by Keane's desperate attempt to snatch a tape-recorder from Gent's pocket; a tape recorder which he'd felt when embracing his companion after an 'agreement' had been made between the two men that for a £10,000 bribe, Gent would do his best to assist the release of a man suspected of being involved in a lucrative robbery.

That tape-recording of the 'agreement' was to get Keane three years imprisonment for corruption.

On the face of it, this incident, though serious, is hardly as sensational as some of the recent corruption allegations surrounding the Metropolitan police: there were no big-time bank raids or silver bullion jobs lying around in the background. But during the trial of Keane at the Old Bailey in 1980, a view of police corruption emerged which was more sensational by virtue of its very ordinariness. For it came out that the suspect in the case was personally known to Keane, and that in his attempt to help him, Keane had simply rung up Gent as the officer in charge of the case, and someone he'd never met before, and tried to find out 'if anything could be done'. In other words, could an early release of Keane's criminal friend be arranged in return for a sum of money. It was a case, as the judge observed of, 'someone going to another person two or three ranks their junior and suggesting that he indulges in a piece of corruption'.

The casualness of this approach, ringing up an officer with whom there had been no previous contact, together with the assumption that it would work, would make complete sense to every professional criminal in London. In fact, nobody that I talked to during the months that John McVicar pulled me and my cassette-recorder round the drinking and gambling clubs of the West End, ever made much of a song and dance about police corruption: it was a small detail in their story.

On several occasions I found myself going back to John and asking how it was that Michael or Lennie or Geoff were still at liberty when the details that I had on record showed that they'd been caught red-handed – 'bang to rights'.

'They must have had a deal,' he'd say. What was the matter with me? Wasn't it obvious?

Even after I'd alerted John to my interest in the subject, in the details of its operation, it often got passed over. Neal, for example, had been describing some of his thefts in the Home Counties, and his subsequent arrest.

'What happened then?' I pressed.

'Well, then we went to the magistrates and copped a plea [pleaded guilty to a much reduced charge]. And got a two hundred and fifty fine.'

'A trade?' asked John helpfully.

Neal nodded casually. 'Mmm. Cost us two grand.'

'The Yard?' John enquired on my behalf.

'Yeah,' said Neal, and moved quickly on to other matters he assumed we'd find more interesting.

I was more successful with Geoff. He'd been a successful con man for 20 years, and even though he'd several times been found in possession of large quantities of stolen cheque books and traveller's cheques and credit cards, he'd avoided all but one small prison sentence. 'How did you manage it?' I asked one night at the Newmarket when he was talking, as he often liked to, about 'the good life' he'd had.

'I just did a few deals.'

'Yes, but how?' I insisted. 'I mean, *what* exactly happens? Do you just pay the man who arrests you?'

I think my frustration must have been showing by this stage because Geoff promptly led me away from the high-stake game of kalooki we'd been watching, into the back room for a mug of tea, and started to spell it out.

'Now, look. Last year. Right? There I am in a police cell. Busted for a wedge of phoney TCs [traveller's cheques]. Now, I know the governor of this nick – Mike Littlewood. Right? Dead crooked. And I've done a lot of things with him before. Right? Now they've all gone out to spin our joints [search the suspect's houses]. Right? I get this young copper, you know, the one in charge of the cells. 'Excuse me officer,' I say. 'Would you see if Mr Littlewood is upstairs in the CID room for me?' He says: 'What d'you wanna see him for?' I say, and I deliberately look a bit nervous as I say it, 'Well, I want to make a-a-a statement. Will you get him f-f-for me.' That's always the first step.'

Geoff was still being patient with me. Why didn't I *know* all this: hadn't John said I was a criminologist? Weren't there lectures on my course given over to 'deals' and 'verbals' and 'fitting up'?

'Anyway, down comes Mike Littlewood.' Geoff's voice went conspiratorial as he peered through some imaginary bars. 'What are you doing here?' he says. 'Listen Mike, you've got to get me out.' I mean it's funny really. There's this young wally thinking Mike's setting me up to make a statement, and there he is doing his best to get me out of it.'

But, as Geoff explained, there were some complications. In a situation like this, the cost of the deal depends upon how much evidence has to be 'buried' or 'lost', and unfortunately for Geoff the search of his house had turned up a parcel of £8,000 worth of traveller's cheques and the paraphernalia needed to change them up. This also meant that other people, such as those on the search party, were in the know, and would have to be paid. But they were wise enough to this sort of trading, and a small team happily came down to take Littlewood's place, and work out the fine points of the deal. Geoff started the bargaining.

'Right. Now I wanna walk out of it *completely*. But there is no way they're going to have that. So I said to them: "You can have a thousand pounds; and I'll duck me nut [plead guilty] to a little tiny one." So they said, "that's all right." And I'm ducking me nut to four hundred dollars' worth in the magistrate's court next morning.'

All this is such well-established practice among professional criminals and certain policemen that the next step is obvious. If the police are going to be given their money – and this is hardly the sort of set-up which encourages trust in credit arrangements – then Geoff has to be got out of the cell on bail.

'So I'm bailed that evening. Straightaway bailed, and later I meet 'em and they get their grand. Met 'em in a pub and gave 'em the thousand pound. Sweet.'

But Geoff doesn't want to let them go too quickly. He's only being charged with having £400 of TCs instead of £8,000, but with his five previous appearances before magistrates, there's still a chance he could get a prison sentence. The detectives tried to reassure him.

'"Don't worry. Don't worry. We'll say you've been right helpful, and we're looking for the person that gave you the TCs. You've given us his [ficticious] name and been very helpful and we expect to make another arrest soon..." and all that bollocks.'

But it still wasn't enough for Geoff. He decided to pay for a bit more security.

'I got hold of 'em just before I went into court. I said "Look. There's another grand in it for you. You gotta go a bit stronger."'

The police duly did their bit about how helpful Geoff had been, and then earned their extra grand by leaving out the one prison sentence he'd ever received when the magistrate called for details of 'previous'. In Geoff's words, they 'buried that one'. The magistrate handed out six months, suspended for two years. 'A bit close' said Geoff.

Nearly all the elaborate deals between police and professional criminals depend upon one key element – the ability of the criminal to contact a detective who is corruptible. The uniformed police who make the actual arrest are not usually thought of as susceptible to bribes: at worst they collude with a system that they know to be corrupt by keeping quiet about their suspicions. In American terminology, they are 'grass-eaters' – passively corrupt – rather than actively corrupt 'meat-eaters'.

In most cases, Geoff pointed out, the vital connection between lay villain and police villain depends entirely upon the system of informers which is at the heart of 'detective work'. It is this which makes it possible for the newly-arrested criminal to ask for a personal meeting with a special policeman.

Although, remembering *Dixon of Dock Green*, it often seems that television and film versions of professional crime have become more realistic, this realism often involves little more than an injection of violence into the police side of the cops-and-robbers confrontation. The actual story-line is still likely to be built around traditional ideas of detection: perhaps not so much the tell-tale fingerprint or the enigmatic message, but still a clue which leads to another clue, and so on, through the narrative, to the final chase and capture.

In fact, detective work, where professional crime is concerned, has very little to do with such clues and everything to do with getting inside information out of informers by methods ranging from reward payments (rewards offered for the recovery of stolen property can be substantial, and anonymity is guaranteed) through to deals which involve dropping other charges, or fixing evidence, in exchange for 'bodies'. Paradoxically, clues or evidence only become important once someone's name is 'in the frame' and the problem of proving the case in court presents itself. It's at this stage, with names already known, that arrests already made, that clues are sought.

When such reliance is placed on informers, then every professional criminal has a double role. He may be a villain who has to be brought to book, but he may also be the highly prized informant who will help detectives to catch bigger fish. The policeman who is faced, then, with a request from a suspect to check with 'George So-and-So at Vine Street' must do so, even if he is perfectly honest and suspects that his colleague George isn't.

The transformation of the informant system into a full-scale pattern of corruption involves one further twist. Once a major professional criminal is face to face with his police contact, he can use his financial power – his ability to bribe – to reverse the intended situation. Instead of the police obtaining fresh information about other serious crimes, they agree to lose some of that which they already possess about the one in front of their faces. The major villain is thus given a licence to operate, while it is the minor criminals who are pulled in to face those charges which are now needed to keep up the conviction rate.

Deals, of course, aren't always going to be possible. Derek, for example, pulled in on one major robbery charge, managed to get through to his police contact and utter the familiar coded phrase, 'Is there anything that can be done?' only to be met by a desperate apology.

'Look, Derek. Look. I'd love to. I'd love to take your money. But I got a Chief Superintendent, a Commander, and there's a cunt in parliament – he's screaming his head off about your lot. I can't do a thing.'

It didn't surprise villains that the police often accepted

bribes. They were being offered a great deal of ready money for looking the other way – and if anything did go wrong, they knew they could rely on the protection and even active support of many of their colleagues. It was certainly obvious to Geoff.

'You get a bootful with 50 grand in notes in it and you say to some copper, 'Well, you've got one of two things. You can nick me and that lot goes back to the Bank of England, or you can face the other way and you're all right for the rest of your life. Here comes my taxi. Make up your mind quick.'

The relation between corruption and the informer system is nicely ironic. For while nobody is more despised among professional criminals than the informer or the grass, it's the very existence of such informers which opens up the police to infiltration. The paradox is nicely pointed by a character called Louis who turns up in a 1936 book about the evolution of a burglar: *Low Company* by Mark Benney. Louis, the chief barman of a criminal drinking club, was always ready to round on anyone who attacked informers.

'*Narks!*' he would exclaim. 'Why you crooks don't know how much you owe to narks. It's the narks who have corrupted and emasculated the police till they can't bring one crime in a hundred to book without receiving information first. It's in giving bribes that the bogeys learnt to take bribes. It's by trading with informers that they've forgotten how to detect crime. For every pound the coppers give to a nark, a thief is able to get away with five from some unprotected householder. If it wasn't for narks, practically every man in this place would be behind bars. They owe their liberty to narks.'

But there's a final twist to the system, which is also part of everyday life for practising villains. With so many deals being done, so many people getting away with it, there have to be some compensating firm convictions of professional criminals for those crimes which attract particular public and official attention, crimes such as Derek's. As hard evidence is unlikely to be readily available in these cases, the police promote convictions by 'verballing' their suspects: attributing statements to them, which nicely reinforce or complement the existing evidence. There's no great secret about verballing: only a lot of hypocrisy. As Geoff insisted: 'Look. A lot of those Crown Court Judges also defend. Right. They go into a court to defend people. Now their approach to police verbals is completely different then. When you meet them in chambers to discuss your case, they'll laugh about it with you. 'Ah. I see there are some verbals here. Good old Inspector Hancock. We've had a lot from him over the years. He should be writing novels.' And they're back in court next week as a judge taking it all dead seriously.'

Obviously, the criminals I met were the ones most likely to give the impression that there was widespread corruption within the police. They were part of that select group of people whose long career in crime had often only been possible precisely because a variety of deals had either saved them from prison, or only put them behind bars for periods of time which could be regarded by them as 'one of the costs of the job'. In this way, they depended on the police and knew that there were times when they had to accept what was coming to them. After all, the relationship between the two sides was going to have to last a lifetime. Even tough-talking Lennie was philosophical in this respect.

'Oh yeah,' he told me, when I asked him one night why he'd not been able to avoid a five-year sentence. 'It's easy enough to do a deal with the Old Bill – but only if they fancy ya. Sometimes you have to go for them. You have to go down. So no good screaming if they done a little bit more to ya than there was to make a fucking case against ya. No good screaming about it. You have to take it and wipe your mouth, cos the next time . . . and there's always a next time if you're a criminal – there's always a next time. You gotta do it the best way you can in the nick. Come out. And then you've gotta start off again. So with that in your mind, you never ever wanna go at the Old Bill. You can go a little bit in the court. But other than that, you don't start screaming 'fit-up' or anything like that . . . because then they'll finish with ya. You're a wrong 'un and they're never no more – when they pick your file up – gonna do business with you. That's for fucking sure. You're cut all roads.'

The files labelled 'Geoff' and 'Lennie' and 'Mike' and 'Les' are regularly picked up. All professional criminals are police suspects. Even if they've avoided prison for a few years by wheeler-dealing, their names are still likely to be known, and automatically linked to those crimes which have involved their particular professional skills.

This doesn't mean that they will be easy to find. Villains, unless they're dope-dealers, do not go in for self-advertisement. They are unlikely to have a telephone, cheque book, credit card or any involvement in the national insurance or taxation system which might require some indication of residence. The flats or houses they occupy may well be in someone else's name to allow for just the recurrent type of emergency that Neal described when he joined in our conversation on how to avoid suspicion.

'I came home one night and I see there's still some of them suede coats in the house. And I'm on suspended, ain't I? Anyway, next morning at half-past seven, 'bang, bang' at the door – I look out the window and there's an old boy with grey hair, with a pail and a ladder. Honest, John. Half-past seven in the morning. What *do* they think? I open the fucking door and watch 'em all rush in past me. Straight to the coats. I said, "I don't know nothing about it." I said, "Look, I wanna tell you something. This flat is not in my fucking name. I do not live here." They said, "Well, we'll have to nick her," pointing at my old woman. I said, "Well, that's what you'll have to do mate. You'll have to nick her." She said, "It's mine anyway." So they nicked her. She went to court next day, she got six months suspended sentence and a two-and-a-half fine [£250]. And, then, John, would you believe it, the Old Bill wanted money off me. For leaving me out.'

But once the police do catch up, they may simply sit around and wait for the next bit of villainy. In Neal's case, for example, they suspected that he and his gang were at the 'jump-up' [hi-jacking lorries] and that the suede coats were part of a recent lorry-load.

'They was on us all the fucking time. I mean they used to set up plot outside Jones's house – he used to live in Plaistow – they used to have three or four motor-bikes. Follow him over to my house. He'd lose them at Wanstead roundabout and come round and there'd already be one plotted on me. We'd have to spend half an hour to lose them, but then once we'd lost them, we'd change motors. We'd have to have old cheap motors knocking about all over the place, change out of our own car, once, twice, and then go and do our business. We never had the brains to think we'd better fucking turn this in.'

The reactions from Lennie and John, who'd been listening to Neal, didn't suggest that he was being marked down for such 'lack of brains'. So I pushed the point a little. 'But you don't sound too bothered by it. Why didn't you stop for a few months? Cover your tracks a bit better?'

'You can't calculate these sort of things, Laurie. You gotta hope ... you say to yourself, you're always saying to yourself when you've got money, 'Let's hope they don't think it's me.'

'But don't you try to lie low for a bit.' The expression was archaic enough to make John flinch, but Neal's attitude did seem so casual as to be almost suicidal.

'Look, Laurie, you've got to understand, a lot of criminals

have got no common sense. They're not brainy. Got a lazy mind. They got a lazy mind.'

John joined in defensively. 'Well, you do that with the heavy [robbery], Neal, cos it's too like simple, it's too simple. It doesn't put you on your toes every day. You get fucking casual, you only get up to the skull [skullduggery] every now and then, and you think "Oh, well, it's easy enough." And it *is* easy, but it ain't easy when you know they're getting clues all the time. It's easy the actual bit of driving down there and going into the jug [bank] or stopping the van. That's easy. But all that talk you've been creating in your little day-to-day world, all that money that's being spent. You give away much more than you need to.'

It was easy at such times to put aside specific harms and injuries, and think of the whole cops-and-robbers scene, not as a confrontation, but as an absurd coalition, with both sides speaking the same language, knowing each other's strengths and weaknesses, permanently engaged in dealing and counterdealing.

Towards the end of the interviewing on the subject, I actively went in search of some antidote to this cynical picture. I made a point of asking each villain if they'd ever come across any 'honest' or 'incorruptible' officers.

There were a few examples where there'd been no deal, but this was put down to the nature of the situation rather than the personality of the officer – too many people had been in the know, or it was a case which had attracted such notoriety that a 'body' had to go 'in the frame'. Only when I put the question to Robert, the all-purpose thief turned dope-dealer, did I get what at first sounded like a straightforward answer.

Well, it's a funny thing,' he told me. 'But there was this one on the robbery squad: he was given four and a half grand once to help out and he gave two and a half grand back.'

'Was it too much for him?' said John.

'No, no,' Robert came back. 'No, he said he didn't need the rest. He said, "You can have that back." He said, "I've got principles." Unbelievable really.'

9

DIABOLICALLY MINDED

In which the author is advised to be careful of Charlie and Ronnie – several people get a lot of treatment – and women are put firmly in their place.

I never got used to the violence. I would be sitting with John in this or that club, chatting to Geoff or Phil or Tommy about some detail of their criminal dealings, flicking the tape-recorder on and off, glancing at my list of questions when – *crash, bang, alacazam* – out would come another horrific story about how Mike had got smashed to a pulp in a fight last night outside the Landsdowne with 'Flaps', how Ted and his brother had 'cut' Big George at the dog track the night before. It was nearly always one villain, or group of villains, against another, and always very bloodthirsty.

At least this stopped me from slipping into the sort of 'lovable rascal' view of villainy which was peddled so seductively by people like Geoff and Les and Mark. Yet even though they claimed to eschew violence themselves, they never showed the least concern when stories of terrible retribution were being bandied about. Instead they pressed for details, nodded enthusiastically at each twist and turn of the lurid descriptions, and in general displayed a quite Torquemadan moral righteousness about the whole business.

Although a few of the accounts were undoubtedly dramatized, particularly when local heroes were sorting out less well-known figures, this was far more than macho talk. Real limbs were undoubtedly being broken: real faces thoroughly cut. Some stories, though, did crop up in different contexts and one or two fights had achieved almost legendary status. What all the conversations provided – and this was no doubt responsible for their graphic detail – was a constant reminder of what happened in this community when you stepped out of line.

None of these people ever resorted to the normal forces of law and order. In some ways they were less likely to need to than many others: their most valuable property was often the wedge of notes they carried in their wallet and the gold watch dangling on their wrist. Although some owned cars, others preferred to hire them from semi-crooked dealers who could waive the usual requirements about insurance and licence, and adjust their books as required to disguise the actual identity of the hirer. But whenever *they* were victims – their house burgled, car stolen, son assaulted, daughter molested – then it was necessary to sort things out for themselves. As I saw on a number of occasions, this could be remarkably effective. When Les lost a valuable radio-cassette system out of his Porsche – a system which delivered just about the decibel level of the six speakers in his pub – he knew exactly where it was likely to be traded, and could go down, find out the name of the likely thief, and threaten terrible retribution for any further aggravation.

Interestingly, the system only seemed to break down when black criminals were involved. Black criminals, I was assured again and again, were different. Very different. Particularly when it came to the central value of loyalty, the vital necessity not to grass your mates.

'The whole thing collapses with blacks,' John explained to me one night. 'Blacks pull each other into line by a balance of terror. "If you grass me, I'll grass you." It's fucking crazy. So much of it. And they're much more individualistic. More opportunist. Incredible. The stories I know about black thieves. Incredible. Exploitative. Cheat each other. And it's all part of their game. Their game is entirely different from the white game. Blacks say, "I'll grass you." They say it. They do it. It's part of their system. There's no feeling that if anyone does it or threatens to do it, that they're out of the school. Different mentality. Entirely different. Something to do with the matriarchal family perhaps. Men get shunted out. Become peripheral.'

So much of the talk about violence among the white criminals concerned grassing. Even though the system broke down from time to time – as it had with sensational effects in the case of armed robbery – endless stories circulated about how particular individuals had been tumbled and subsequently dealt with. Down at the Landsdowne, Neal saw himself as a scourge of grasses: he'd personally rooted out a number for special treatment. He had a nose for them:

'Cos I can pick you out wrong 'uns. I can tell you they're wrong 'uns – I can tell you who's wrong 'uns, that's guaranteed without no fear of contradiction. I'll surprise you John, an' all. I can smell it and I can tell ya. By listening in to conversations and putting two and two together and listening to people in drink. I can hear things go in drink that could never be fucking right. It takes a criminal mind, and I've trained my mind – I trained my mind to get tuned right in. Exactly as they talk, I can tune in on them. There's Jekylls out there in the pack and I can smell 'em.'

Violence or the threat of violence wasn't restricted to grassing. It was also standard treatment for all those types of internal deviance which were covered by the ubiquitous phrase 'out of order'. Even though credit was instant in this community and could be extended for long periods of time, it was out of order not to pay gambling debts after a couple of warnings. It was distinctly out of order to behave noisily or aggressively when you were on someone else's patch or manor: in his spieler or drinking-club. It also covered any sort of attention being paid to another man's wife or a woman who had through regular association become 'his'. And it was particularly out of order to pay attention to a woman whose man was in prison – a taboo which could virtually ensure her a period of purdah lasting as long as the sentence.

Although almost any professional criminal could expect to be involved in physical violence at some time or another during his career, only the gangsters made violence their trade, their speciality. Most of their actual money came from involvement in rackets, from ownership or control of a variety of illegal services: prostitution, pornography, drugs, gambling. They rarely initiated any of these rackets – in fact gangsters were routinely described as lacking the brains or intelligence for any sort of entrepreneurial activity. But neither, as I had always assumed, did they simply muscle in on existing rackets and extort 'protection' money. In many cases their protection was positively welcome. It was a form of insurance against trouble, and against outside competition, which could hardly have been otherwise obtained. In two of the gambling clubs that I visited, the resident gangster had his own table in the corner from where he could amiably survey the scene. His comfortable position and share of the profits rested entirely upon reputation, upon his known capacity, for what, even in this aggressively minded community, was regarded as extreme violence. On several occasions, I tried to discover the moral limits of this violence: what exactly would be regarded as going too far? But I had little success. The question didn't seem to make much sense. Gangsters did violence much like robbers robbed. What would it mean to ask about the top limit for robbery?

Neither did there seem much likelihood of putting the question to a gangster. They weren't exactly a category like hoister or con man: other villains might refer to gangsters, know who was one and who wasn't, know which rackets they were into, which clubs and groups of people they looked after. Gangsters themselves, though, didn't seem to have quite the same sense of their identity. A few did favour a sartorial double-breasted style and a mode of speech which owed rather more to Sunset Boulevard than Commercial Road. (Ronnie Kray, for example, had emulated Al Capone even to the extent of hiring a private barber and cultivating a taste for Italian opera.) But in general they regarded themselves more as local businessmen who occasionally had to intercede on behalf of their clients when outside interests or a spot of internal trouble threatened to break up the established order of things.

Even in more favourable times, I couldn't imagine John taking me across for an introduction and an interview. So Lennie was purely a piece of luck. Although not someone who would be described as a gangster – more an 'all purpose thief', to use John's phrase – this short, squat, slightly punch-drunk villain had been into a great deal of violence himself, had tangled with gangsters, and retained an evident belief in his own physical prowess. Most importantly, he wanted to talk. John reluctantly agreed to set it up, although, as I soon realized, there was an element of mild maliciousness in his choice of venue.

For while Lennie was ideal company in a pub or drinking club, his loud, aggressive manner and fondness for using the word 'fucking' with heavy emphasis upon the first syllable meant that he was less suited to a more refined environment. And John had thoughtfully selected for our meeting place one of the most fashionable and indeed trendy new restaurants in the West End – L'Escargot in Greek Street. Snail motif on the fitted carpet, framed scientific descriptions of the mollusc on the wall, a chocolate version of the gastropod to munch with your coffee – and television producers or directors or presenters or moguls at every other table.

I was nevertheless still interested enough in my 'moral limits of violence' question to start by asking Lennie for his view on the most outrageous of all recent gangsters. Relying upon a principle of primary teaching I'd once learnt at a college of education, I asked in a tone of quiet reasonableness:

'What did you think about the Krays, Lennie?' I knew in a second that the principle wasn't going to hold.

'They were *fuck*ing terrifying,' boomed Lennie. '*Fuck*ing terrifying.' He looked for support to John who nodded back encouragingly over a spoonful of fish soup (yes, go on, Lennie, as loud as you like, we can really wind Laurie up tonight).

One or two of the nearby diners seemed to be already nervously bracing themselves for some vivid examples.

'And the Richardsons?' I persisted in my quiet voice. 'Charlie Richardson?'

'*Ooooh*!' went Lennie, scrunching his body as though a passing waiter had just thrust a dagger deep between his shoulder blades. 'Be careful. Be careful. That's the thing with Charlie. See, Charlie's diabolically minded. Charlie's got a bit of a brain. But Charlie's game is to slip people into ya.'

Whether or not the atmosphere was actually getting just a little too heavy for even John, I can't say, but he certainly switched the tense as though to reassure those on neighbouring tables that Charlie's threat was purely an historical one.

'Oh yeah. He *was* marvellous at using people.'

Lennie was grammatically undeflected. 'And with Charlie – it's majority decisions. He wants majority decisions. He waits till he's ripe for you and then slips someone in.'

John decided to pursue comparisons with the Krays. 'Were they different sorts of gangsters?'

'Different thing altogether. Different kettle of fish.'

'Yes, they had that edge with everyone, didn't they, Lennie?'

'Oh for sure. They had a *fuck*ing edge.'

John seemed anxious to outdo Lennie in his appreciation of the Krays' mysterious 'edge'. He joined in eagerly with his analysis. 'Cos you felt, oh my fucking Christ, it's all the way with these, didn't you, Lennie? Out of *nothing*. It could be just out of nothing and yet they'd *kill* ya. And there's very few people would go that far. I mean, there's a lot of gangsters that would go a bit outrageous.'

'Reggie's not so bad. Reggie's not so bad. Reggie? Talk to ya. Not so bad. It depends how much of a doer you are yourself. Ronnie's a different kettle of fish. I tell you the reason why. This is what makes him different from other people. Ronnie, see, wouldn't be fucked about by people. If he thought they was frauds, he'd never say nothing. And if they'd been naughty and had to be cuffed – he wouldn't cuff them like you would a little kid – wouldn't just go "smack". "Behave yourself." Oh no. No cuffing with him. He wouldn't just knock a mug out and leave it at that . . .' What on earth, I wondered, did it mean to say that Ronnie wouldn't 'just' knock a mug out? But there was little chance to climb inside one of Lennie's bulldozing monologues. You had to hang on till the end.

'No, he wouldn't just knock a mug out. Oh he'd just *fuck*ing . . . just completely *fuck*ing . . . like you know, until he'd got his satisfaction, until it had steamed out of him.' Lennie gave a sudden and violent impression of a large ape beating its chest to indicate the savagery of the assault. 'Aaaaargh! Aaaaargh! Aaaaaargh!' His fists rained in on himself. 'See, like he's off his head. Really go over the brink. *Go over the brink* and do more damage than he should do being a gangster.'

Even though it was almost concealed within Lennie's evident enjoyment of Ronnie's unpredictable ferocity, this idea of going over the brink was what I'd been looking for. I wasn't going to get another opportunity. I decided to risk the sensitivities of the L'Escargot customers.

'Why was it more than a gangster should do?' I asked.

'Cos gangsters don't ever act that way. They only do what they got to do and go as far as they got to. You've got to have people respecting you, but never in fear of you. They done what they done because they thought they'd get away with it. But they pushed people to the brink, so people was absolutely in fucking fear of their lives with them. You never felt at ease with them. And when you lose that, you've lost everything. I'll tell you why.'

I could see that John was leaning forward: he wanted Lennie's opinion on the Krays as much as I did.

'Cos you'll never get the gist of nothing. You'll never get the context of nothing. When the people around you have got to watch their Ps and Qs, when you've just got yes-men, you are in danger. You are in *absolute danger* – cos there's no one gonna say to you: "Be careful of so-and-so." And why didn't anyone say it? Why? Rhyme and reason? Why? People are too frightened of you. So the Krays never got their cards marked. They had the West End at their mercy. They could have run the West End. But they never had the fucking brain to manoeuvre.'

'Was they stupid then, Lennie?'

'Reggie wasn't stupid.'

'Don't you think so?'

'No.'

'No? But he can't talk can he.'

'Doesn't matter about talking, John. He had the right mind to do it. The right frame to do it. They didn't need to go no further. They was right for it and they was on to it. *But they went a bit too fierce.*'

I knew what he meant by a 'bit too fierce'. As part of my preparation for this interview, for my introduction to violence and gangsterdom, I'd reread John Pearson's dramatic account of the Kray twins *The Profession of Violence*, in particular the murder of Jack 'the Hat' McVitie. It was a powerful desensitizing exercise.

Ronnie . . . grabbed him, locking his arms behind him, and

Reggie ... was holding Bender's carving knife. The room was silent.

'Kill him, Reg. Do him,' hissed his brother. 'Don't stop now.'

McVitie ... stood there looking very bald and gaunt, his long face sweating.

Instead of answering, Reggie pushed the knife into his face below the eye. The butchering followed as McVitie sank to his knees. According to Ronnie Hart, Reggie stabbed his stomach and his chest and finished by impaling him through the throat on to the floor.

John and Geoff had told me earlier that Pearson's book was inaccurate and oversensational. (Perhaps the Krays would have been better served by their original choice of biographer – Truman Capote.) But neither denied the actual killings, or seemed to regret them greatly, except for the sort of expedient reasons that Lennie was now advancing.

It was something I kept coming back to with John. Surely he couldn't condone that sort of behaviour? Well, no, not exactly condone, he'd say, but then it was villains fighting villains. People knew what to expect if they stepped out of line – if they took liberties. Much of the time gangsters didn't need to do any actual fighting. People got to know, credited your reputation, backed off a little at the last moment. It was this mutual ranking, this business of determining your place in the hierarchy of toughness which fascinated both Lennie and John. It was a regular exercise, a human handicapping system, which was persistently discussed in spielers and drinking clubs. You need to be up to date on macho ratings, or you might accidentally find that you'd gone that little bit too far with the wrong person. Lennie, busy nibbling a lamb chop which looked more like a pigeon wing in his pudgy hands, found space to mark John's card about a man called Irving. A new threat.

'Very, very wicked man to cross. You can frighten him. There's people he's nervous of, but if he has the edge on anybody – they're fucking gone. I mean he is a wicked man. I've seen him . . . You know what I mean? He methodically – I've seen him – he methodically beat someone to fucking death. And properly and all. And no fucking messing. Methodically break your arms and legs and break your fucking shoulder-blades and everything. Your jaw – the lot. And teeth, and eyes out and all, I'm telling you, he fucking . . .' Again a passing waiter drove a knife into Lennie's back and he scrunched forward over the plate. 'Ooooh . . . yeah. A most callous man. You've got to be very careful of the callous people.'

I was not very good at suppressing my real feelings of horror at these stories, and in particular at the casual, unquestioning way in which they were received by people who I knew from other contexts were generous, amusing and self-critical. Although Lennie could use words like 'callous' to describe a particular villain's predilection for extreme violence, it seemed bleached of all moral colouring: it was simply a category into which some people fell – not unlike 'athletic' or 'outgoing'.

I could sense that John, as at other times, wanted to find himself a space somewhere alongside Lennie, but a space which was clear of any of the liberal debris with which I was always littering our late-night conversations. 'It's funny, isn't it, Lennie, how you can get edged into these things – edged into a kind of bullying. You know, you get pally with someone, but then they start taking liberties. I was in the nick with Brownie. Remember Brownie, Lennie? In the kitchen. And we were washing up. And he had a tool [a knife – a potential weapon] in his hand. And suddenly there was this nasty bit in his voice. He was trying something on. So I thought, I thought I've got to swallow this here, cos I can't do anything.

'But the next day I watch him and he goes into the karzi. And I go in. I shut the door, you know, like the glass doors. Shut the doors. So I said, "Pete, I don't like this. You're saying funny things. You're getting out of order. There was a little thing the other day I didn't like."'

John gave Lennie a taste of the stare he'd then put upon Pete. He waited for a couple of seconds to get the effect. 'And then I see the funk in him, Lennie. I see the funk in him. He didn't just speak to me, didn't say, "Well John, if that's the way you feel, I don't really want to have a row with you because you're not a bad fellow." Like there might have been between mates. Without any funk. Know what I mean? I see the funk in him. See the funk in him.'

It's incidents like these which restructure relationships: from now on, it's known that John has got the edge on Pete. No fight needs to take place, only the subtle recognition by one person that the other is frightened by its prospect. The language of these 'ranking' exchanges is oddly understated considering the threat of extreme violence which lurks behind it. John complains to Pete that he doesn't 'like' his attitude, that he's saying 'funny' things, that there was a 'little' thing he hadn't liked. It all adds up to an ultimate phrase of condemnation taken from the language of the school debating society – I'm sorry but you're 'out of order'.

Much of the time, of course, I was coming across villains whose reputation was already established – who'd proved themselves in the past, and could now sit back and rely on that fact to save themselves from trouble with newcomers. I knew from John that Lennie had seen off a few notorious gangsters on the way to his present status. I asked him about them. If he wasn't a violent man himself, how could he take them on?

'Well, you see, gangsters always do have 90 per cent in their favour. They never do it when it suits you. Always when it suits them. And you get it out of the blue, you see.

But I've seen a lot of them. And a lot of them are one-punch fucking big geezers. I see a lot of them and they're bullies. But it's more than bullying when it comes to the real *fuck*ing thing.'

Lennie's conversation was already into the ring and facing up to the imagined opponents ... every '*fuck*ing' delivered like a straight left.

'You've got to have a *fuck*ing big 'eart. I've seen one or two of them gangsters go. I've seen one or two people with right faces go. And I've thought, "I've gotcha." I'm having a one-to-one with a big fella at the Casino. And I thought to myself, "I've done you, you cunt." I could see the fear in his eyes. And I started talking to him then. Doing a Cassius Clay. Talking. Quiet. Saying, "I'm gonna smash you to *fuck*ing pieces, you cunt."'

John was also at the ringside now, laughing along with Lennie's relaxed sense of superiority over his opponent, while I noticed with relief that the staff of L'Escargot seemed to be creating a modest *cordon sanitaire* around us. For although the two tables on our immediate left and right were empty, the dining conditions at the far end of the room looked positively cramped.

'"Oh yes," I said. "What I'm going to do with you, you mug," I said. "You wait." *Bang. Bang. Bang*. And then all the others come at me. But they didn't put me down. Cos with this lot, if you go down and stop fighting, they kill you. Well, you gotta do what you gotta do, and I used to carry a little penknife on me. And I could give someone some treatment. *Phoooooooo*. I was on 'em like a fucking dose of ... if they said anything to me I was on them like a dose of salts, sticking it right into their fucking heads."'

It was becoming far more graphic than I wished, but still perfectly within the limits for this type of conversation. John hadn't given me a single one of those 'sit still and listen quietly' glances which he reserved for episodes where he thought it likely that I might want to raise some moral quibble. And Lennie was so busy with his penknife by this time that he might well have missed the Count Basie Orchestra arriving to serenade our table.

'Like a dose of salts. About twenty times. I had one of them on the floor bleeding profusely with blood spurting up the walls, and then I done two more. I do for *him*.' He stabbed vigorously at the small airspace between his head and John's. 'And I did for *him*.' Stab. 'One in the throat. And one in the fucking eye. And I crashed everything in there, every bottle, every glass went into their fucking heads. I made a double certainty of that. And then the Old Bill went and put things about me that I was dangerous.' Lennie's incredulity and pride were blended with a panache they'd have envied in the kitchens. 'They said, "Approach this man with caution." That's on my record. I've seen that record. The screws showed me that. "Approach this man with caution: he's a dangerous man."'

Despite the mayhem and carnage which had been piling up before us in the last ten minutes, John was able to pull back to the original question. I could see he was still fascinated by the psychology of gangsters, by those people who, as he insisted when we'd been talking to Phil, were quite different to armed robbers because of their emphasis on combat rather than risk. Bank managers and policemen who'd been involved with him in the past might have thought the distinction somewhat academic, but it was clear that John felt himself miles away from those whose whole livelihood rested upon their known ability to fight and win.

'Have all gangsters got the bully in them, Lennie?'

'Yes, they have. And they can't beat a man with a bit of brain. Once you've got a bit of brain, John, they can't beat ya, cos you're gonna be too much for them, cos you'll outread 'em, outthink 'em.'

'They don't take real risks, like thieves, do they?'

'No, they don't. And I notice they don't fight each other.'

'They talk about each other? "He's easy meat." "He's a nellie."'

'Oh yes. But they don't fight each other. They help each other that way. Although they don't say so. They pick on nice easy ones to fight.'

'So what have they got? What makes them gangsters?'

'*They can do it cold-bloodedly*, John. That's all. There's always that edge in their favour. People know they can do it cold-bloodedly. That's what makes them fearful. And the rest is done by propaganda.'

It was difficult to maintain the hard edge of the conversation over desserts: the sorbet and chocolate fudge pudding seemed to incline everyone to nostalgia. Lennie started talking about a villain he'd once worked with on a very profitable and long-running job. As far as I could gather, it involved taking charge of parcels' delivery at King's Cross. Both of them had got prison sentences for their part in it, but Lennie's mate had insisted on going round the actual prison still pleading ignorance. The governor had come to visit Lennie to see if he felt the same way.

I wasn't quite certain why Lennie was telling this particular story. Usually prison tales were taboo. But as the coffee and chocolate snails were dispatched and Lennie's voice began to rise again, I began to suspect that it was going to be another celebratory anecdote: something to reaffirm common identity with John; a shout of approval for unashamed, unqualified villainy.

'So the governor comes in. "Ah Greenwood," he says to me. "Do you also say you're innocent in this matter?"

'"*Innocent?*" I said. "*Innocent, be fucked*. Course I'm not innocent. I've had it good now for five years. Plenty of *fuck*ing money. Plenty of *fuck*ing women. Good time I've had. So *fuck ya*."'

I'd been right.

I didn't doubt that Lennie had had 'plenty of fucking women'. And by this time I wasn't too surprised by the fact that it went hand-in-hand with having had 'plenty of fucking money'. Women, rather like bottles of champagne or gold watches, were acquired when there was money around. Sometimes the actual transaction was almost as straightforward. Villains who'd just come out of prison after a long stretch might well be provided with a woman as well as a couple of grand in readies, while on a more day-to-day basis there was a number of women who could be counted on to provide working criminals with regular sexual services.

Such women were not thought of as prostitutes. They came from the large collection of 'club girls' who performed a whole variety of semi-legitimate waitressing and hostessing duties round the clubs in the West End. For many of them, this meant getting paid for sexual activities, but as the clients were likely to be rich businessmen, foreign tourists and visiting Arabs, this was generally regarded not as prostitution, but rather as a minor confidence trick. Stories abounded of how this or that girl had left her client bound hand-and-foot to the bed eagerly awaiting some masochistic pleasures, only to find that his 'strict schoolmistress', with a sadism more subtle than he'd envisaged, was going through his wallet before making a speedy departure. Clients like this were the classic 'mug punters' of a hundred villainous stories, and the women who 'took' them were allowed at least honorary status within the subculture.

Although the criminals who enjoyed sex with such 'club girls' might also pay for their services – albeit in kind rather than cash – they found no difficulty in believing that their involvement was of a completely different nature to that of other clients. After all, they were in the know. Nobody could mistake them for 'johns'.

It was not a subject I found easy to pursue, but I never felt that there was much more than a temporary and grudging regard for such women among professional villains. In fact, much of the sexual talk in which they featured was of a relatively perverse kind, with stories of elaborately stage-managed encounters in which the climax seemed to consist of the male participants being physically stimulated and finally brought to orgasm by the combined ministrations of several women. This type of sexual activity was somehow regarded as more liberated than any other, and was favourably contrasted with the routine monogamous sexuality of the world and his wife.

I'd tried during my meetings with Geoff to learn something about the extent to which criminals' own wives were involved in their husbands' lives. Again, it was not a subject on which anyone wanted to talk. But it was clear from the stories in which wives featured, particularly those involving the arrest and subsequent trial of the protagonist, that their principal task was to keep well out of everything while all went well, but then to act as alibi, messenger and general fixer when trouble arrived. It was hardly an enviable position. They were unlikely to receive any great financial advantage from their husband's villainy: most of this money was spent on gambling and drink. Neither did they share any of the excitement of the escapades: all they saw of the action was limited to the traumas of early-morning police raids, long and humiliating visits to police stations and jails, frantic efforts to raise money for bail and bribes, followed by the prolonged imposed purdah which was the consequence of their husband's imprisonment. By way of compensation during his absence, they could count on little more than a whip-round from the other criminals to help out with immediate expenses, and perhaps some oversentimental letters from prison which addressed them in unrealistically romantic terms and promised that this would indeed be 'the last time' – 'I just can't wait to be back home with you and the kids once more.' If, by any chance, luck went the other way, and the husband, far from being jailed, was able to pull off a major coup, then a wife was likely to find herself abandoned for a companion who could act as a more effective display-case for the villain's new-found affluence.

On the face of it, only the details of this discrimination set it apart from the routine sexism of many other social and matrimonial arrangements well outside the world of professional crime. But it rested upon a sense of maleness which was tightly bound up with the cavalier attitude towards interpersonal violence. Often the philosophy behind this was banal: there was much talk of men being naturally aggressive, of basic animal instincts which shouldn't be repressed, of the law of the jungle, and the survival of the fittest. What was more interesting, however, was the view expressed with varying degrees of explicitness that the readiness of its members to resort to aggression made the professional criminal culture one of the very few places where real men – proper men – could be found.

Active aggression was so tightly bound to maleness that it was even possible to use it as a compensation for homosexual predilections which otherwise might have been regarded as the antithesis of masculinity. Ronnie Kray was only the best-known example in this area. 'I'm not a poof, I'm homosexual,' he would boast, and according to his biographer, Pearson, referred to 'pansies' with the same cockney contempt with which he pronounced the word 'women'. His reputation for violence, and his proprietorial and slightly sadistic attitudes towards his 'boys', aligned him so well with the values of his culture that consideration of mere gender could be overlooked. 'Beautiful,' he would say, pointing to his latest boy. 'Don't you think he's beautiful? Don't you wish he was yours?'

All this emphasis on masculinity made for a great deal of

posturing in the clubs like the Lansdowne. Only rarely did you have a chance to display actual aggression: for the rest of the time you had to rely on looking tough. That meant thumbs held cowboy-style inside belts, large measures of spirits ordered with laconic gestures, hearty two-handed Italian greetings, enough heavy gold jewellery to resink the *Mary Rose*, and skin-tight tee-shirts to set off the pectorals. Not everyone took part in this status game – weedy, pale-faced con men, hoisters and burglars scuttled between the colossi – but when it came to muscle-flexing, many professional criminals had a good few inches start on 'straights' because of the obsessive attention they'd given to weight-lifting during their years inside. ('Some of them', John once wrote to me sadly, 'would rather put an inch on their biceps than take a year off their sentences.') But for many, the very best proof of all that you were thoroughly male was provided by the attentions of attractive women.

'I wonder why women like criminals so much?' John asked Lennie, down at the Landsdowne, a few nights after our noisy and violent meal at L'Escargot. 'I wonder what it is?'

It was no problem at all to Lennie. 'Cos they get a bit of flair from them. They like a bit of excitement. People that have been sheltered all their life and go to convents, it's in 'em, see. Bascially, it's all based on animal instincts. They absolutely like to be beaten. They like to be beaten, some women. They absolutely like to be beaten. They like to be brow-beaten. I mean you get a girl, common girl, that abhors violence. She just works in a factory, comes home, and if her husband pushes her around a bit, she would feel that she would never want to talk to him again. And yet there's women that come from a good background that like a clump now and then. They do like a clump. And there's an old saying, that you treat ... an ordinary woman you treat as a lady, a whore you treat as a lady, and a lady you treat as a fucking whore. And that's basically what it's down to. That's exactly what it is. It's excitement. See. The excitement. Women always think there's more to it than there is. You can give 'em a basic story and their imagination runs away.'

Lennie was crasser in his account than others might have been, but I didn't see or hear much in houses, or clubs, or restaurants, to make me believe that he'd have encountered any serious opposition to his views in this culture.

Indeed, as he bulldozed on with stories of how impressed women had been by this and that piece of villainy, I remembered another incident from Pearson's study of gangsters which provided a cruel commentary upon the fate of women who were less gullible. Frances O'Shea had by all accounts been an exceptionally bright and intelligent woman when, at the age of 21, she married Reggie Kray. After a tragic two years in which she simultaneously tried to free herself from the pampered status which he pressed upon her, and come to terms with the anxiety she felt about his routine villainy, she committed suicide. Her father observed, 'It was a horrible thing, but all I could think of was how those bastards destroyed my daughter.' While Reggie honoured the occasion with a poem which, if it did nothing else, admirably captured the other-worldly position which this culture reserved for women who were 'loved':

> If I could climb upon a passing cloud that would drift
>   your way
> I would not ask for a more beautiful day
> Perhaps I would pass a rainbow
> With Nature's colours so beautifully aglow
> If you were there at the Journey's End I would know
> It was the beginning and not the End.

Life would hardly have got easier for Frances. The 'sentimental madonna' status from which she excused herself could only, as the years passed, have degenerated into that of unwilling accomplice. Lennie provided just that complementary scenario as he struggled to produce, for John's benefit, a check list of the qualities needed by the real professional criminal.

'You see, John, those young kids can do it because they haven't any fear. But too many people get the fear in them as they go through life. And they crumple up. I mean, I was turned over every week. Every solid week I had the law round my house. Looking everywhere. Pulling stuff around. Questions. Dates. Times. Everything. To me it meant nothing and I could just walk out and forget all about it. But my old woman, it destroyed her fucking mind. It absolutely destroyed her mind. She was such a nervous wreck. And yet at first she was as strong as me. I thought even stronger than me. But in the end it got to her. Took her own life. Got to her.'

He paused, seeking another explanation to lift some of the responsibility from his own shoulders. I could see John hesitating as well. He knew enough women from before and after his prison sentence to recognize the tragic chronology of most of their lives. At first innocent girl-friend – the object of sentimental adoration; and then their gradual transformation over the years into disturbed, demented, even suicidal, spouses.

'You see, John. She always wanted to be a young girl. Frightened of getting old. And it didn't sort of suit me. I was always "Jack the Lad" and I suppose I was out with the birds and she heard different things about me.'

Another fact of nature occurred to him and he warmed to it.

'I'll tell you this, John. A man can always go looking at a woman. A woman's got so many years – and it's *bump*. A man can go out and get women when he's fucking seventy.'

John nodded. 'I suppose so, Lennie,' he muttered.

'You see, John, women are just great for some of their time – and then that's the end of it.'

'Yeah. That's triffic, Lennie. Thanks a lot.' He leant across me and flicked off the cassette recorder. Enough was enough.

That same evening we were back at the Battersea flat. Unusually, John had hung on a bit – had not rushed off to find another club, or link up with a few old mates in what I understood as some sort of nocturnal exorcism of his previous identity as an observing sociologist, a way of making amends for treating this culture with insufficient empathy.

'D'you mind?' I asked, bringing out the recorder.

He shrugged.

'What d'you really think about all that tough talk and violence? You don't think of yourself as like Lennie, do you?'

'Oh, yeah. It's embedded in your identity, isn't it? Your esteem and your image is all bound up with it. You encounter situations which question it and you just react emotionally. If you don't react, you feel dreadful afterwards.'

'But don't you sometimes feel dreadful when you have reacted?'

I was remembering a few weeks ago when John had come back to the flat after an incident on a nearby running-track. Some sort of fight. He'd been challenged and there'd been a violent set-to. Although he'd not been noticeably injured, he'd seemed shaken by it. I'd stored it up to use on an occasion like this.

'Yeah. I'm in ... I'm in between, yeah, in between the stools now. Mmmm. Yeah. Cos I've had about ten incidents over the last few years. Violent confrontations. And none of them have been ... very ... I'm not, you know, I don't look back on any of them with any ... it's a very ... difficult thing.'

'But you still do it, like so many other criminals, because

you think you're being challenged in some way.'

'All criminals do.' He moved with some relief from the personal to the general. 'It's that grey area where how much power you've got pushes back the moral code – gives you more scope to do what you want to do. Power is how much respect you can induce in other people. I've spent 17 years in prison where you're dependent entirely on physical prowess. What you get is determined by that. You can't allow any encroachments on that, cos you pay dearly for them.'

'But you've been out of prison for three years. So why go on, now, dealing with "encroachments" in the same way?'

'Because if you're a criminal and you're damaged or harmed, you never complain to authority. Criminal identity is rooted in not calling the police. That's much more deeply ingrained than responding violently. I'm trying to extinguish ... I'm sort of tackling the violent response because it is a problem. The other thing – not going to authority – is not a problem. That will always be there. That attitude to authority. *That's what's properly criminal.*'

10
BLUE LIGHTS AND SLOW MUSIC

In which the author hums some now familiar tunes — gets caught up by the rhythm — and records a swansong.

I now felt that I recognized many of the theme tunes of this culture. Some, indeed, were so familiar from interviews and discussions and late night tittle-tattle that I could have sung along with them when the first chords were sounded. I was practically word pefect, for example, on *omerta*, that rather grandiloquent Italianate aria about the value of silence and the disgrace of informing, with its sad contemporary coda about the scourge of supergrasses. I was equally at home with the Spanish strains of *macho*, or rather with that particular English version 'matcho', where the emphasis shifted away from the sheer expression of physical strength and sexual virility towards a pride in one's ability to take 'pressure', face risks, and stay cool.

At a less lofty level, I could recognize the obsession with knowing how the odds were stacked in every social situation; the delight in any scheme or game, however childish or surrealist, which subverted authority; the respect granted to displays of cold-blooded violence; the insistent depiction of women as romantic sweethearts, sexual playthings or wifely accomplices; and the vision of the rest of the population as a greedy ignorant mob of 'mug punters' who were simply asking to be taken.

It wasn't too difficult to maintain mental reservations about most of these attitudes. In fact, I found it mildly reassuring that my repeated exposure to them had had so little effect. I hadn't exactly expected to turn into a criminal as a result of my meeting so many villains and sharing so much of my social life with them, but I'd been on guard against any dramatic increase in my general level of cynicism, materialism, or tolerance of violence. This, unfortunately, was not the end of the story. For, although I felt relatively untouched by the familiar themes of this culture, I found that I was much more easily seduced by the insistent rhythm, the specific pace of life, which accompanied them.

Some nights I could have sworn there was a competition among them to see how late it would be before anyone dared to say that they simply *must* go home and get some sleep. We'd be reaching some natural climax to the evening at, say, two o'clock in the morning: the wine had been finished, the kalooki game we'd been watching had wound up, the club showed every sign of closing for the night. Just the sort of moment in normal company when one person can be relied upon to give a small token yawn, a slight symbolic stretch of the arms, which allows another to mention home and another to pile in with 'Gosh, is it two o'clock already?' and yet another to add, 'Yes, have to be up early tomorrow.'

But no matter how hard I searched the faces around me at the Landsdowne or Newmarket or Professional Artists', I could rarely find any signs of imminent departure or a slow-down in the social pace. Like little children, Geoff and Phil and Les and John and Lennie were always wonderfully adept at finding ways to stay up later. Once one set of toys had been packed up and the way left clear, then out would come another plaything. Sometimes we merely moved clubs – there was actually a chronological sequence here – so that one went to J. Arthur's in the Fulham Road between 12.00 and 1.00, the Jacaranda in Kensington after 2.00 and Dino's in Notting Hill any time after that. (As this arrangement seemed to hold true when we were with different sets of villains, I often wondered whether such clubs were otherwise quite empty outside these preferred hours.)

And if it wasn't 'another club' which was used to keep the

evening going, then the ante might be raised, the sense of ending dispelled, by drawing upon any from a long list of stimulants. First on the menu was usually champagne. Clubs seemed to know about this late night or early morning predilection, for no sooner was the £20 note pushed across the counter than an ice-bucket with a bottle of Moet was on its way. (It was, I learnt later, the *customer*'s price rather than the establishment's: champagne was *the* drink with which to con 'mug punters': the £20 only transaction ensured that no villain was thought for a second to be a member of that group.)

After champagne came 'coke'. I always declined that – not out of any great moral sense, but because even in the most bohemian of clubs it meant disappearing into the lavatory for a moment with a ten pound note, a razor-blade, and that little precious parcel. I already felt quite clumsy enough when it came to such routine matters as ordering drinks and parking cars, not to wish to add a Woody Allen impersonation to my repertoire. On occasions there was 'speed' as well. Simplicity itself. Just lick your finger, dip it in the packet, suck off the powder as though it were childhood sherbet, and you were guaranteed to be awake and buzzing for the next eight hours.

Not that these late night sessions were exactly bohemian. The champagne and the coke and the speed, much like the lunchtime cannabis at the Horse and Groom, were given little more than perfunctory attention. There was certainly no mystery attached to any of them, no sense that they might provide the opportunity for introspection or mellow philosophical speculation. In fact, it was not considered appropriate to draw any attention to their effects: it was macho to show that you could handle internal pharmacological risks as readily as you could situational ones. The real point was, that as long as champagne corks were being popped, coke snorted, and speed licked, you were still awake and moving and ready for action.

Everything was expected to be sharper and that little bit quicker than among the straights. You spoke quickly, filling all the space with words. In fact, nothing so much marked out wallies (and in particular those rural and northern wallies who had been typically encountered in jails around the country) than slowness of speech. Gestures were rarely casual or languid but controlled from the wrist, and chiefly used to emphasize the briskness or efficiency of the operation which was the subject of the talk. You didn't look when you could glance, and you never 'faffed' around when ordering drinks, sitting down, pouring wine or lighting cigarettes. You stayed alert, moved smartly from point to point, drove fast, made snap decisions. There was a contagious frenzy about it all which could quickly become irresistible. Everyone else was left standing at the lights. It was what Mark Benny called, on the basis of his own long experience of this world back in the 1930s 'the very spirit of the underworld . . . not the titillating externals of booze and bawdry . . . but . . . *the fierce pulse of anti-social life*'.

The anti-social pulse was critical not simply because it marked off villains as somehow stylistically superior to those around them, but also because it was tied in with their philosophical view of the world, with the idea that if you stayed sharp and alert, used your eyes and brain more than those around you, then you would be able to spot all the myraid flaws and cracks in the surrounding social fabric and devise exact techniques for exploiting them. Phrases like 'ducking and diving' and 'looking for clues' were standard responses to questions about how villains were now making out. Often the clues you discovered were gaps in security, but the thief and the con man also depended a great deal on finding a psychological weakness – something which would hook a plutocrat into an elaborate swindle, or lead to a security guard describing the route to be taken by a van-load of bullion.

Personal advantage didn't even come into it on some occasions. Ducking and diving has intrinsic merit. A fortnight after I'd first been introduced to the club scene, John, now settled back into London life and trying to catch up on a couple of decades of popular culture, took me along with a group of friends, including a con man called Dave, to see a Bob Dylan concert at Earls Court. Although Dylan was still rumoured to be in his God phase, the concert was popular enough, and I gathered that Dave had only got the tickets as a favour from the ticket-tout Stan Flashman (who seemed to be a personal friend). We advanced to the barrier with Dave waving the tickets aloft. 'This way, this way,' he went, turning quickly to the man on the gate to explain that there were, 'Six of us – yes, six of us,' but there was no need to worry because he was in charge. And he certainly looked as though he was. 'Ah yes,' he went. 'There you are John. Right, Laurie, this way.' All the time, dodging and weaving between the other ticket-holders, blocking the barrier for a moment and then pushing one of us through. Finally, all six of us were on the other side and could move forward to take our seats.

I noticed as we went that Dave was casually pocketing a ticket which he'd managed to retain while all the chaos he'd induced had been rolling round the barrier. 'What on earth has he done that for, John?' I wanted to know. 'There's six of us, and he'd got six tickets. What did he want to cheat on that for?'

'Must be inadequate socialization,' John had muttered as we made out way into the area.

It wasn't always as easy to find the little gap through which you might wriggle. One night in the Landsdowne, John had been talking confidently about a millionaire who looked likely to put up some money for another McVicar film, when Lennie butted in to warn him against being overconfident. Millionaires weren't pushovers. You had to be specially sharp to get an angle on them. 'Remember, John. A man that has money never has to spend none. Never has to spend a penny. Everybody wants to wrap him up. You always have to be careful with men with a lot of money, cos they're never gonna give you nothing. They just *fuck*ing use ya. That's for sure. I've watched the way they work, see. But there's ways into them. There's a chink there. You gotta watch for the chink, and when you get a chink in the armour, you *know* you've got 'em.'

According to the philosophy of the professional criminal, this chink or clue is always there: millionaires, like the rest of the 'aristocracy' or 'upper class,' are always on the cheat, are forever ducking and diving themselves, in the same way as their counterparts at the other end of the social scale. Lennie was determined to assure John of that:

'Millionaires are looking for *fuck*ing perks . . . They're all at it. They're all at the *fuck*ing cheating game. Every one of them's at the cheating game. No matter where they are, the rich are cheating. All you gotta look for is what they're cheating at. And once you know what they're cheating at, you've got 'em. Because you can move in.'

This was far from being a radical philosophy. Villians have no apparent political wish to usurp the 'upper class': they are delighted to be able to exploit the chinks in its armour, and by so doing establish that they are equally in the know, equally clever at cheating.

'I'm on a par with them, brain-wise,' insisted Lennie. 'I'm not giving myself a gee. I *fuck*ing know I am. That's for sure.'

Sometimes the symmetry between the two groups, the upper classes and the professional criminals, was even more explicit. Geoff, the con man, was almost mathematically precise about it:

'Top-class villains are about . . . a narrow one per cent of the population – maybe half a per cent – rather like the one per cent in the opposite direction, the real hierarchy of the establishment – the aristocracy and the royal family, that epitome of honesty and understanding.'

If this social theory was going to be maintained, then it was obviously critical for villains like Geoff to separate themselves from all other criminals who regularly filled the courts and the jails and the tabloid headlines. 'How can I tell who's a "top-class villain" and who isn't?' I asked him during one late-night session.

'You take the one per cent who go on robberies and never harm anybody. That's top-class. Those who go on robberies and never shoot anybody. But the people there think they're going to be shot. They're top class at it. They wouldn't hurt a lamb. They're actors and grafters. And that's their game and they're fucking good at it.'

I must have looked unconvinced. The categories didn't seem so watertight to me. 'Professional robbers aren't always gentle,' I ventured.

'There's robbers, Laurie, top class, who *if it's an old person, they won't do the tie-up.* In case they have a heart attack. Never been guilty of even hurting anybody. The gun's got no bullets. You've got to understand it and be a bit more compassionate with them. Not in the same category as people who smash an old lady over the head. They're the top one per cent.'

For Geoff and others, the worst pain of imprisonment was the fear of contamination induced by having to spend years with people with whom they felt no affinity, who fell well outside this elite percentage.

'Look at me last time, Laurie. I never hurt anyone. I'm in a top-security fucking nick with three or four murderers on each landing and fucking dangerous people come out of fucking Rampton, or Parkhurst nuthouse thing, finishing off long sentences for God knows what. They put me in with *them*.'

Along with this notion of some kind of dialectic between

the two groups who were in the know went an abhorrence of the middle ground, not just of the Bingo-telly-*News-of-the-World* lumpen working class, but also of the standard middle-class lives presumed to be led by the rest of the population. Geoff turned on me fiercely when I asked him if he ever saw an end to the life he led at present.

'Who wants to be a fucking Norm, Laurie? There's lots of people that I know, grew up as kids, got a job in a factory and became cab-drivers – *cab-drivers*. Fucking cab-drivers who've bought a little house in Neasden and now they've got fifteen fucking grand in the bank and they go to all the social functions and they're "big-timers".'

There was a precision about Geoff's invective: that fifteen grand in the bank was made to sound like a statistical finding rather than a guess.

'They're rich then, aren't they? In their little suburban homes ... Cab-drivers with a little fucking house that ain't worth two bottles, put up any old how, don't even fucking stand up properly – they get the velvet curtains up and start holding *The Times*.'

I knew from past conversations that Geoff would now go on towards a highly developed conspiracy theory which he shared with other villains – an account of how the one per cent at the top bamboozled the rest of the population, how they sat around and devised techniques (which included white bread, lead-poisoning and keg bitter) for keeping them undernourished and sickly and therefore quiescent. The world was stuffed with mugs. They believed anything they were told. You had to be a proper villain to know otherwise.

New examples of this conspiracy were continually being found. Even though the lunatic DJ Les for example, didn't follow Geoff through every twist and turn of his elaborate theory, he was always on the look-out for further proof of what 'they' were up to.

'Look at the Royal Family,' he announced portentously

one night at the Landsdowne. 'It's marvellous the way they kid people. Honestly, it's incredible. I watched the Duke of Edinburgh the other night talking about the Royal Yacht. Fucking *yacht*. Fucking *yacht*. It's an ocean-going liner. And do you know what they have on board? They have a hospital unit permanently on duty with all the best equipment and surgeons. And d'you know what they have the audacity to tell people what it's for? D'you know?'

Silence. (Everybody at the Landsdowne could spot Les in rhetorical mood.)

'So that in times of war they'll be able to use the yacht as a hospital ship to pick up wounded seamen. That's what they tell people, and they stand for it. When I pull that kind of line, they give me ten years. Honestly, this country is run by some of the most clever, sophisticated heads that it's possible to have. And what's so incredible is that very few people tumble. They just don't know.'

I didn't get the impression from Geoff or Les, or anyone else, that they felt that there was anything particularly *unfair* about aristocrats and plutocratic practices. There wasn't any active resentment or sense of inequity. The Royal Family had been 'ducking and diving' successfully. What Les wanted to draw attention to was the legion of wallies who failed to notice what was going on. Not that notions of fairness or equity or justice were absent from this culture. There can be few groups of people who have such a pronounced sense of these matters who speak so much of principles and of what is fair and reasonable. There was altogether quite enough moral self-righteousness around at times to wallpaper a seminary. Mike, for example, belonged to a rather smart health club in Mayfair; one of those executive gymnasiums where you're expected to exercise for half an hour before retiring to your own cubicle for a special massage and a large gin and tonic.

Recently the proprietors of this club had found out from someone (probably a police-officer client) that Mike had done a spell in prison. He'd been promptly excluded. 'I mean. Is that fair? Because someone's been inside.' This was directed at me, not John. Surely as a criminologist I should be properly outraged? 'Because of what someone's done in the past. Don't you think it's diabolical?'

Well, yes. On the face of it. But hardly enough to have anyone searching for the National Council for Civil Liberties number. For all the crowd round us in the Landsdowne, who were looking equally shocked at the behaviour of the health club, knew full well that Mike was still an active villain, had been out robbing that very morning. There were excellent contemporary reasons for excluding him from any straight club. It didn't make a scrap of difference. The essential moral point was that the club had no way of *proving* this – and so Mike was innocent. Not just technically, but actually.

This sense of 'fairness' was derived from what might be called a judicial morality – it was the product of dozens of courtroom experiences where a fair result was not one in which the jury and judged matched verdict and sentence to the actual crime, but in which people played their parts correctly. This meant that accomplices did not implicate each other in their statements, that there was no hint of any informing behind the scenes, that the police kept to any deals which they had struck up with the defendants before the case, and went easy on this or that piece of evidence or left out a conviction or two when 'previous' was mentioned. It meant that proper weight was given by the court to carefully assembled, but bogus evidence about the defendant's newly acquired employment, his reconciliation with his wife, his recent period of psychological stress, the uncharacteristic lapse back into old ways which the present offence represented.

There were just three types of prison sentences, argued Geoff. 'There's prison sentences where people are innocent – can you imagine that one? Can you imagine it? Then there's prison sentences where people have a fair crack, where you have a word with a few people, make the right decision to plead guilty or not guilty, get some 'extenuating', and it works out, boom–boom–boom, and it's a fair sentence. Sweet. You can do it easy. A hundred miles an hour. But if you get a sentence that ain't fair – one that ain't fair, one that sets you against people – then that's quite different.'

Despite all this solid agreement on what really counted – on the values of *omerta* and *macho*, the tactics of ducking and diving and looking for clues, the conspiratorial world view, the notion of what was fair, the fierce rhythmic accompaniment – despite all this, there were many occasions when it was possible to look round a typical late-night club scene and find the whole enterprise distinctly precarious.

For even though there were plenty of such clubs where villains might gather and feel at home, this was, compared to earlier times, a relatively rootless group of deviants. No longer did it have the firm geographical base of the East End to fall back upon. The language, with its combination of Yiddish and rhyming slang, still owed a lot to that source, and there might still be the odd parent hanging on in Bethnal Green or Hoxton, but otherwise this happy ecological niche, where professional villains could expect at least some tolerance, if not respect, from family and neighbours, was only a folk memory.

Neither was there anything very familial about the structure of the London underworld which might act as compensation. Although gangsters such as the Richardsons and the Krays had been, and still were, likely to rely upon close kin for support, this was hardly an embryonic *Cosa Nostra*. Temporary alliances between mutually interested parties were the best that could be expected. Indeed, Lennie and Geoff both complained to me on separate occasions about the lack of organization and consolidation in British professional crime. People were 'too selfish'. They were 'only in it for the money'. They didn't invest, as did their American counterparts, in lawyers and accountants and property. When the crunch came – as it had with the police use of supergrass against the armed robbers – they simply had to take what was coming to them. There was no organized resistance.

Certainly, there was no great strength to be found in numbers. Although I had initially been surprised by the coherence of this culture, the degree to which different types of criminals felt an occupational, social, domestic, and even political affinity, over the six months I'd toured round London I had never got any sense that there were more than a couple of hundred fully paid-up members. That, of course, did leave large numbers who deliberately stayed outside to avoid suspicion, and those up and coming 'cowboys' who might not have been welcome. But overall it was difficult not to agree with the journalist who suggested to me on one occasion that 'Villains are almost due to become a protected species. The police are on to them. All those computer records on how they work, all those supergrasses and new ways of interrogation. And the profits aren't big. I doubt if altogether they take as much in a year as half a dozen big inside City frauds. There are probably more professional criminals pass across our television screens in a single year than actually roaming the streets of London.'

For extra measure, there is something resembling a death wish among some such villains. Not just in the lack of care they take to cover their tracks, or in the reckless way in which 'profits' are gambled away, but in the self-dramatizing which they bring to their roles. It's difficult to complain about the slightly crude melodramatic treatment of professional criminals in the media, when actual robbers and con men and gangsters appear to go out of their way to increase their own visibility, and thus their likelihood of detection, by trying to live up to such images. I didn't meet anyone who'd emulated Ronnie Kray's impersonation of Al Capone, but there were a number of people whose clothes and demeanour seemed more calculated to draw attention to their potential villainy than disguise it. After a very short time, I found them instantly recognizable in straight clubs and restaurants; as though they were acting out a little stage version of the 'underworld' for the benefit of the patrons at adjoining tables.

If I'd recently endured a long bout of conspiratorial theorizing from Geoff or Les, I was even inclined to turn their version of the world on its head, and see such professional criminals as the ultimate 'mugs', in that this active collusion with the available villainous stereotypes allowed the rest of the population to go on believing that they indeed were the real enemies of society. Meanwhile, the subtler and less visible and more significant pieces of corruption and fraud could continue, either undetected (because police resources were concentrated upon the pantomime villains) or, if detected, likely to find that any moral censure which might have come their way was already firmly attached to the traditional blackguards.

It was all part of what Edward Alsworth Ross, back in 1907, called the 'lack of imagination' which prevented most of us from recognizing that there were now new villains around who were less explicit than the ones we were familiar with from the popular papers and the detective novel.

> The stealing and slaying that lurk in the complexities of our social relations are not deeds of the dive, the dark alley, the lonely road, and the midnight hour. They require no nocturnal breathing with muffled step and bated breath, no weapon or offer of violence. . . . The modern high-power dealer of woe . . . sins with a calm countenance and a serene soul, leagues or months from the evil he causes . . . The hurt passes into that vague mass, the 'public', and is there lost to view.

It is always, claims Ross, whose highly polemical book *Sin and Society* boasts an introductory letter from President Roosevelt, the 'crass physical act' which is heeded by the public and not the 'subtle iniquity'. We insist upon our crime being dramatic: 'Villainy must be staged with blue lights and slow music.'

It's ironic, then, that there are criminals themselves who, while otherwise protesting most vehemently about the marginality of their illegalities, continue to strike the very villainous postures which help keep them firmly centre stage.

What was it that led certain people and not others into this complex and contradictory culture? I'd spent quite enough of my academic life marking essays on the causes of delinquency to make certain that I always included a question about getting started in the standard interview.

All of them, predictably enough, had been involved in petty delinquency of one sort or another, and then there had been an escalation. They had gone a little bit further than those around them. But, as with the armed robber Phil, the reasons seemed unclear:

'Well, I suppose I got started in Hastings with the young Mods. About '63. We started being a bit physical, fighting other boys, and then – I don't know why – two of us broke away and sort of did the local supermarket.'

'Was that when you started to feel you were tougher or more daring than the other boys?' I asked. (These were early days in the interviewing, and my questions still had this check-list sound.)

'No, not really. No. I used to steal cars, you see. I learnt to drive stealing cars,' he looked at John. 'As *you* know, it was always left to me to fucking steal the car. Stole six cars in one day. For other boys. It was like a yo-yo.'

'But you didn't think you were going to be a criminal. It was just fun.'

'Well, I suppose I was a bit inveigled in by fucking cunt called Joey. He was the governor in Clapham Junction. He had some skills. But it was still mostly audacious – not heavy. I would go into a jewellery shop and grab and just run. Run away with £3,000 worth of jewellery and sell it for two hundred quid. And then into a bank when people were paying money over, sort of grab it and just run. Didn't even have a car.'

Neal had started on his career as an 'all-purpose thief' in much the same way – running into jeweller's shops and snatching rings. Geoff had gone out with a few mates on the Tubes just nicking what they could see and had then drifted into a gang of professionals who were 'at the whiz' and learnt the trade from them.

Lennie didn't seem to understand the question at first. 'I just started,' he said.

'But did you ever work?'

'Work?'

'Like for a firm, in a factory – like that?'

'Naaaaaw. I never *worked*. What d'you mean? You mean ordinary working?'

'Yes.'

'*Never.*'

Most succint of all was Derek. As soon as John and I had settled ourselves on the divan in his back bedroom, I'd asked him somewhat regally:

'Can we begin by enquiring how you got started?'

'Well. I met 'im.'

There were so many contingencies in the accounts, so many lucky and unlucky breaks, accidental meetings, unexpected offers of illegal work, that all I felt sure of in the end was that each of the villains I met had at least three common characteristics which inclined them towards their present life. All of them had been particularly audacious delinquents and had as a result got a glimpse of how easy it was to prey successfully upon the legitimate world: the bluff put around by the agents of social control about the likely penalties of crime and deviance had been well called. Their audacity had also guaranteed big cash rewards: there were many echoes in the accounts, of Mark's delighted cry: *'I thought, this is a piece of cake. All this fucking dough you could get. I don't wanna work twenty-four hours a day.'*

The only other shared feature was the impact of the first spell of detention. Given their wholesale involvement in delinquency of all kinds, this arrived quite late on in their careers, at least late enough to allow them to realize that it was by no means an inevitable consequence of deviance. This meant that prison or Borstal could be read as straightforward 'cost', as something you had to endure as part of your style of life. It was this acceptance, more than any other, and the ability to find others inside who took a similar view, which marked the end of apprenticeship and the entry to the occupational culture.

Of more immediate relevance, though, to the men I met, was the question of whether or not to try and get out after ten, 15, or 20 years at the game. This culture, unlike the occupational culture of the accountant or the schoolteacher, was likely to have permeated every aspect of their personal, social and family lives. It probably meant that they had never taken a normal job, never known security or respectability, and had handed over years of their actual existence to prison authorities as the prize for at least part of their relentless deviance.

It was the 'cost' of prison which was raised most often when I asked for a reason for quitting. By this stage of their careers prison was beginning to hurt. Most of the men I talked to were between 35 and 45 and the prospect of another ten years inside was becoming difficult to face.

Derek was keeping away from armed robbery for the moment, turning to what he called 'a bit of buying and selling.' The risk was just too great – although the temptation remained.

'It's so easy to do it. And I think, well, I could go and do it tomorrow. But if I fell next time, it's the end of my life, innit? You know, there's only a certain amount of bird you can do, I suppose. It's like saturation, innit? I've done 14 years out of the last 22. It gets to a stage where you think that's it. Although you know it's still as easy to do.'

Along with the deepening shades of the prison house went the knowledge that you were also now even higher up on the suspect list. Your criminal record grew with you and made it more and more difficult to operate. A committed villain like Lennie was quite prepared to take that in his stride. It was a price you had to pay, almost an additional part of the sentence to be worked off before you could get back to the game. 'Getting out' for him only meant looking as though you were 'getting out'. He delivered his advice on the subject to John with almost Mosaic certainty.

'Let me tell ya, John. You must start right. This is how basically you can do it. You must be out of the limelight, you must be out of the mind's eye, you must be out of the limelight. You must *not* associate. You must always tell anybody and everybody that you are a straight person. You've got to be prepared to sacrifice. Everything you do a little naughty you've got to say, "Well, I've got to cover for this." And in the end they'll *know* you're going straight. *Cos other people will tell them*. When they know that, they're off your *fuck*ing back. They think, "Well, leave him alone." They're off your back. They *are* off your back. But it takes *fuck*ing years to do it. Years of just managing and scraping by. Years of it. And then you can go to work again.'

Lennie had hardly followed his own advice: his present complex involvements were some way from being 'straight', and others found it no easier to take. It wasn't just that you would miss so many aspects of the culture. If, like all those I interviewed, you'd been a successful criminal, then you could hardly shuffle off into trivial illegalities, or domestic and social isolation, without feeling that you were seriously evading your responsibility to other less successful colleagues. Professional crime is a group affair: each highly successful criminal will have several others who depend to some extent upon his courage, strength and skill for their own livelihood. How could Geoff, for example, follow Lennie's advice and stop 'associating' when he was persistently hunted down:

'I get calls at the tennis club. "Come on out. What ya doing?" They all think I'm looking for a clue, you see. But I haven't got any clues. Only silly jobs. Things I could do and hate doing. Things, that if I get busted, the value ain't there.'

But the telephone calls at the club were the least part of it: 'In between all this I get people coming up to my flat everyday: burglars, scallywags, the old die-hards. I've always earned money for them over the years. Still hanging in. Come up. Cup of tea. Endless tea-pot going on in the mornings. First one's Jim – three buzzes, *Bzzz–Bzzz–Bzzz*. I know that. It's Jim again. Jim comes up. He's got fresh rolls from the best bakers in London. *Guardian* for me and *Mirror* for himself. Next thing, another ring at the door – little scan – another guy comes up. I'm going through the motions. To keep everybody happy. They all work for me and I haven't got a fucking move in the book.'

As usual, Geoff had an anecdote to capture the full absurdity of the situation, the depths to which, he, as the master con man, had now been forced to sink, if only for a couple of months.

'Guy came in the other day, Laurie. What do you think he said? Serious guy. I couldn't believe it. He said. "Look," he said. "I've got something." I said, "What?" "Listen," he said, 'I've got *a million pounds worth of luncheon vouchers.*"'

I knew the obvious person to talk to about 'getting out'. The fact that John had 'done it' was a regular subject for conversation. It wasn't seen as wholly admirable – in fact Geoff had come up with a conspiratorial hypothesis about it which enjoyed general agreement. His argument was that the authorities – the establishment – knew that they had pushed too hard with him. His sentence had been too long for what he had done and so it was time to make amends. 'Somebody', said Geoff, 'was fair to John.' And it was this 'fairness' which had convinced John it was time to stop his villainy.

It was no longer easy to talk to John himself about such a subject. There was a passive agreement between us that everything could be discussed except those matters which might bring up the question of the sudden end of our collaboration. Not until six months after my final interview with an active villain did we eventually talk about what had happened to him since we'd first met in the Salisbury and set off as two sociologists to examine professional crime.

We were back in Battersea again. Across the kitchen table. I asked him if he minded the cassette-recorder.

'No. Why not?'

'I'm sorry we couldn't agree about . . .'

'More me than you.'

'Well, it seemed that you . . .'

'Yeah, well, it still resonated. And I couldn't take the way you summed everything up. As though it was all unlike the rest of the world – universities, people in the City.'

'And I thought you were further away from it than you were.'

'You can take intellectual decisions about it. I could see it for what it was. I could. When you're young, you've got a few things going for you in crime. You've got more liberty ahead of you. But as the years go on, you get more convictions, you've got less time to play with. You've got less life. And you begin to edge a bit more. You become more unscrupulous, more fearful, more treacherous. Not just you, but the people all around you. And I can see that intellectually.'

'But emotionally . . .'

'Emotionally, it still plucked. Your emotions take a certain shape. They condition how you're going to feel in whatever circumstance. And that's what makes it hard to unshackle a criminal identity. You have to take all the emotional pressure to go back to your ways – you can't do it in one, it's not like giving up smoking or drinking where you can keep a check; you get caught up again in subtle things. You can be aggressive in so many ways you don't realize – lean on people, raise the ante. It is a bit overwhelming – crime.'

'You feel you're away from it now.'

'I just don't want to stay trapped in any particular mentality, any set of emotions. I don't want to be cut off from understanding by my own ego.'

In a way I wanted to welcome him back. Assure him of the reality of the world which existed outside professional crime. But he effected his own re-entry.

'Yeah, I can't quite feel the emotional tug of it anymore. I find I've lost that. I'm an onlooker now. Like I thought I was at the beginning of all this. Like you've *always* been.'